AF817633

TABLE OF CONTENTS

APPLICATIONS OF GRAMMAR /

Principles of Effective Communication

Revised Edition

TEACHER'S MANUAL

Christian Liberty Press Arlington Heights, Illinois

49646 R9/07

2007 Printing

A publication of

Christian Liberty Press

502 West Euclid Avenue

Arlington Heights, Illinois 60004

www.christianlibertypress.com

Written by Edward J. Shewan

Copyediting by Diane Olson

ISBN 978-1-930367-29-6

1-930367-29-5

Printed in the United States of America

Introductory Note to Teachers

This teacher's manual has been written to help the teacher accurately and efficiently check the answers given by the student for most of the exercises in the student workbook. As a rule, only the answers to the exercises appear in this manual; however, when necessary, the original exercises have been repeated along with their answers. For the teacher's convenience, page numbers have been included after each "EXERCISE" heading in the Text Key section of this manual, indicating where the exercises may be found in the student workbook.

■ *Course Exercises and Requirements*

Since the first three units of this course integrate grammar and composition, many exercises require the student to creatively write various compositions. The teacher, therefore, should be judicious when grading these compositions, checking to see if the student has followed the guidelines given in the appropriate lessons and in this manual.

In regard to Unit 2, each student is required to write a 1,500-word research paper. The teacher should check page 6 of this manual for specific requirements. The next section, entitled "What Parents Should Know About Plagiarism," should also be consulted.

In other units, the student is asked to write sentences using his or her own words or to provide examples of the grammatical subject discussed in the lesson. Sentences and other answers given for these exercises will vary from student to student and may not coincide with the answers given in this manual. In such cases, the answers provided in this manual are for illustrative purposes and for theoretical comparison with the student's answers.

In several lessons—especially the Unit Review lessons—objective answers are required. The student's answers, therefore, should match or closely match the answers given in this manual.

This course has fifteen tests, which means that some of the units have two tests. The following course and test schedule will guide the student in completing the workbook exercises and taking the tests. Note that the test or tests should be taken after the material for each unit has been completed. The only exception is Test 5, which covers "Common Fallacies" in Lesson 29 of Unit 3.

Units		Weeks	Requisites	Tests
1	**Thinking and Writing**	*4 Weeks*	Exercises and 750-word essay[a]	Tests 1 and 2
2	**Writing a Research Paper**	*8 Weeks*	Exercises and 1,500-word research paper[a]	Test 3
3	**Writing an Article of Opinion**	*4 Weeks*	Exercises and 1,000-word article of opinion[a]	Tests 4 and 5
4	**The Mechanics of Good Writing**	*3 Weeks*	Exercises	Test 6
5	**Colorful Writing**	*3 Weeks*	Exercises	Test 7
6	**Nouns and Pronouns**	*3 Weeks*	Exercises	Tests 8 and 9
7	**Verbs, Verbals, and Participles**	*3 Weeks*	Exercises	Tests 10 and 11
8	**Five Other Parts of Speech**	*3 Weeks*	Exercises	Test 12
9	**Phrases and Clauses**	*3 Weeks*	Exercises	Test 13
10	**Sentences**	*3 Weeks*	Exercises	Tests 14 and 15

a. The student should complete the workbook exercises, writing assignment, and test(s) for each unit before proceeding to the next unit. Due to the amount of material and the effort required, Units 1–3 must be executed in this manner to successfully complete the course work.

What Parents Should Know about Plagiarism

Christine Pelton, a high school biology teacher, discovered that twenty-eight of her sophomore students had plagiarized their biology projects from the Internet. She gave all of these students zeroes for their assignments. The school administration even admitted that the students deserved to get zeroes. Then, the students' parents complained. In order to placate the parents, the administration required Miss Pelton to reduce the value of the project so that the penalty for cheating would have less effect on the final course grade. As a result of this unfortunate deference shown to cheaters and their parents, Miss Pelton lost control of her classes and resigned in protest.

We can applaud the integrity of Miss Pelton. We must grieve, however, at the cheating itself as well as the responses of both the parents and the administration of the school. Plagiarism is a serious offense. By definition, ***plagiarism is the act of taking the words and ideas of others and presenting them as one's own***. Sadly, this offense is becoming all too common in schools today. Standards of academic integrity have eroded considerably in our nation.*

Before we become too judgmental of this public school dilemma, however, we, as Christians, need to examine our own hearts and tend to our own homes. Plagiarism and academic cheating occur even in Christian environments, and Christian home schools are not immune. As the parent/teacher of your home school, you must be diligent in discipline and oversight in order to deter this behavior.

We must be realistic about the impact of sin in our own lives and in the lives of our children, and take nothing for granted. As the Scriptures teach us, judgment begins with the house of God. Therefore, we must be harmless as doves and wise as serpents (Matthew 10:16) regarding this issue. We must not simply assume that this offense could never happen in our home.

One of the greatest threats to academic integrity today is the temptation offered by the many free research paper Web sites on the Internet. By way of illustration, type in the search field of your Web browser the phrase "free research papers." You may be shocked at the number of Web sites offering free research papers and essays on a wide range of topics. The proliferation of these sites has been nothing short of astonishing.

Because of the growing milieu of academic cheating in our nation, as well as the growing apathy toward it, a homeschooling parent must be fully engaged at every step of a student's research project (*See Unit 2*). The following are a few steps that you can take to develop a "culture of accountability" in your home to prevent plagiarism in this regard.

- Require your student to check in with you before, during, and after each step of the process of writing a research paper.
- Do not let your student move on to the next step in the process until you are fully satisfied that he is doing his work correctly and honestly.
- Insist on being fully informed about your student's electronic and hard copy sources, and check the pages from these sources cited in your student's paper to be sure your student has documented these sources accurately.
- Verbally quiz your student during the process of proofreading his early drafts and his final draft to ensure that he is mastering the material he is researching and not just downloading or copying someone else's work.

---

* In his Web article entitled "The Importance of Writing" (<http://www.plagiarism.phys.virginia.edu/essays/The%20Importance%20of%20Writing.html>), Louis Bloomfield, Professor of Physics at the University of Virginia, reports the extent of this offense and offers ways to maintain our intellectual integrity.

➢ Finally, take the time to educate yourself about the problem of plagiarism.

To learn more, read pages 37–40 in the student workbook. You should also look over the following Web articles: "Using Sources" at <http://www.hamilton.edu/academics/resource/wc/usingsources.html?print=yes> and "Plagiarism: What It Is and How to Recognize and Avoid It" at <http://www.indiana.edu/~wts/pamphlets/plagiarism.shtml>.

■ A Final Word

The primary objective of this manual is to help the teacher ascertain whether the student fully understands the concepts taught in each lesson. The teacher, therefore, should use discretion in checking the student's work with the material given in the course. The manual also includes various notes to the teacher which deal with certain answers that may need clarification or an extra measure of forethought.

May God bless you as you guide your student in sharpening his composition skills and developing his grammar proficiency. It is our prayer that this course will encourage your student to use this gift of language to glorify God and further His Kingdom.

TEXT KEY

Unit 1 Think Before You Write

LESSON 1: WHAT IS MY GOAL?

✎ **EXERCISE A (Page 4)**

E 1. How to arrange a bouquet of flowers
N 2. A terrifying experience while traveling to a strange place
A 3. Why Christians should run for public office
D 4. What Victoria Falls (in southern Africa) looks like
N 5. A biographical sketch of the Apostle Peter

✎ **EXERCISE B (Page 5)**

Answers will vary.

Teacher: Students are required to write a paragraph for each of the following writing goals: *narrative, expository, descriptive,* and *argumentative.* Each paragraph should be at least three or four sentences in length.

LESSON 2: WHO IS MY AUDIENCE?

✎ **EXERCISES A and B (Page 7)**

Answers will vary.

LESSON 3: WHAT IS MY TOPIC?

✎ **EXERCISE A (Page 8)**

T 1. Conflict in the Middle East
T 2. A character sketch of Patrick Henry
T 3. How to defend your faith
S 4. Sir Winston Churchill
S 5. Wycliffe Bible Translators
S 6. New York Stock Exchange
T 7. Trials of the pioneers
T 8. Making origami flowers or birds

✎ **EXERCISE B (Page 8)**

Answers will vary.

LESSON 4: WHAT IS MY STANCE TOWARD THE TOPIC?

✎ **EXERCISE (Page 10)**

Answers will vary.

Teacher: In two or three paragraphs, the student is required to describe his own *worldview* and how it will affect his writing. In one paragraph, he also needs to explain how his *attitude* will affect his writing.

LESSON 5: HOW AM I GOING TO SUPPORT MY TOPIC?

Teacher: Due to the amount of material given in this lesson, it may be divided into three separate lessons. Each of the following exercises give opportunities for students to use various methods of gathering, classifying, and arranging information that will support their topics.

✎ EXERCISES A, B, and C (Pages 12, 13)

Answers will vary.

LESSON 6: WRITING STRATEGY

✎ EXERCISE (Page 17)

Answers will vary.

LESSON 7: TOPIC BUILDERS

✎ EXERCISE (Page 19)

Answers will vary.

Teacher: After filling in the blanks with words of their choice, students are required to write a paragraph for each of the four topic sentences given, using some or all of the approaches discussed in this lesson.

LESSON 8: UNITY AND COHERENCE

✎ EXERCISE (Page 24)

1. (d.) <u>Keep in mind that you are a spiritual creation.</u> (c.) You must nourish the part of you that the Bible describes as your "spirit." (b.) Just as there are all types of food for the body, there is food for the soul or spirit, "spiritual food" (1 Corinthians 10:3). (f.) But not just any food will meet the nutritional demands required by your spirit. (e.) Just as there is "junk food" that can rob your body of essential nutrients and can turn a healthy body into an anemic one, there are all types of "spiritual junk food" that can wreck your spiritual health. (a.) If you don't eat the right spiritual food, you will starve to death or you will seek any nourishment that promises to satisfy your hunger. (Gary DeMar, *War of the Worldviews*, pp. 65, 66)

2. (c.) <u>The neutrality myth has been used by secularists to keep a Christian perspective of the world out of the arena of intellectual thought.</u> (b.) Unfortunately, many Christians have fallen in the trap by assuming that a subject can be studied without any reference to religious presuppositions. (a.) Christians are told, "You can develop your own *personal religious* convictions, but you cannot bring these *personal religious* convictions to the classroom. You must be neutral like your professor." (Gary DeMar, *War of the Worldviews*, p. 24)

3. (d.) <u>Postmodernism has broken the stiff neck of humanistic modernism.</u> (b.) As man seeks consistency in his anarchy, he will watch his futile autonomy trickle from his clutches into a pile of dust at his feet. (c.) It is the church's duty now to answer the world's wail of despair. (a.) Throughout all ages and into eternity, man's deepest yearnings will only be filled in Christ. (Gary DeMar, *War of the Worldviews*, p. 44)

LESSON 9: TRANSITIONAL MATERIAL

✎ EXERCISE A (Page 27)

At the age of twenty-five, after conducting a successful caravan trade to Syria for a wealthy widow by the name of Khadija, Muhammad accepted Khadija's offer to marry her. Despite the fact that she was fifteen years his senior, the marriage proved to be a happy one for both. The couple had two sons who died in infancy, and four daughters. Almost nothing is known about this stage of Muhammad's adult life except that it seems his good reputation and respect constantly grew among his people.

It is during this time period that many have speculated Muhammad grew more and more discontent with the paganism and idolatry of his society. This was not unique since several other prominent citizens of Mecca denounced the paganism of their homeland and declared their faith in the one true God, including Jews and Christians. In accordance with the customs of the pious souls, Muhammad began the practice of devoting "a period of each year to a retreat of worship, asceticism, and prayer." Some say he would spend the whole month of Ramadan in a cave on Mount Hira two miles north of the city of Mecca, living on meager rations and meditating in peace and solitude. (Norman L. Geisler, *Answering Islam:The Crescent in the Light of the Gospel*, pp. 69, 70.)

1. Underline words and phrases in the paragraphs above which serve as transitional devices.
2. Which type of order is used primarily in the first paragraph above? ***chronological***

✎ EXERCISE B (Page 27)

Even in view of this assault of liberalism on the educational institutions of the church, the progress of modernism was uneven and was not obtained without great struggles. ***X***[1] It gained greater strength in those churches that were Armenian in their theology, or which had no creeds of any consequence to guide their theological development. ***X*** [*It made relatively little headway in some of the churches and met with great opposition in others*.] Although heresy made itself felt in the Presbyterian Church USA in the closing years of the nineteenth century, this church, with a group of stalwarts for the faith at Princeton Seminary, continued its testimony for the historic faith until well into the twentieth century; it was not until the appearance of the Auburn Affirmation in 1923, and the ensuing reconstruction of Princeton Seminary at the close of the decade, that liberals could be said to have officially taken over this once great church. It met even greater resistance in the Southern Presbyterian Church, and in some branches of the Lutheran Church in this country. The conquest of Princeton Seminary by the forces of liberalism was a strategic victory, and of great consequence for the evangelical church in the nation, for this school had given forth a scholarly defense of the Gospel for over a century.... (C. Gregg Singer, *A Theological Interpretation of American History*, pp. 180, 181.)

LESSON 10: RESOURCES AND WRITING

Teacher: Note that the exercises in this lesson (pages 28 through 33) have not been marked off; however, each student is required to complete the charts on page 29 and write an essay that is approximately 750 words—carefully following the instructions given in the text.

1. If the student places the sentence at this point, it would be *acceptable*; although, the latter position is *preferable*.

LESSON 11: UNIT REVIEW

✎ EXERCISE (Page 34)

1. The ***thinking*** process precedes the ***writing*** process.
2. The key to effective writing is ***a deep understanding of the greatest story of all time***.
3. Writing involves an ***ongoing*** process which includes using your mind, making decisions, and organizing your thoughts ***before*** you write them down in a meaningful and orderly way.
4. What are the five ways in which your raw material may be arranged?
   a. ***Chronological Order***
   b. ***Spatial Order***
   c. ***Order of Importance***
   d. ***Comparison or Contrast***
   e. ***Analogy***
5. List the four basic writing goals.
   a. ***Narrative*** (to tell a story)
   b. ***Expository*** (to inform or explain)
   c. ***Descriptive*** (to describe someone or something)
   d. ***Argumentative*** (to persuade or convince)
6. Expository writing explains an idea, gives a definition, ***gives reasons for something happening***, or ***presents facts on how something works*** in a detailed manner.
7. Descriptive writing describes a ***person***, ***place***, or ***thing***.
8. ***Argumentative*** writing tries to persuade or convince.
9. List the four stages of argumentative writing.
   a. ***Opening stage***
   b. ***Confrontation stage***
   c. ***Argumentation stage***
   d. ***Closing stage***
10. When considering your audience, what four questions must you answer?
    a. ***What do they know?***
    b. ***What don't they know?***
    c. ***What type of language do they use?***
    d. ***What biases or convictions do they hold?***
11. A ***subject*** is an unrestricted, familiar area of knowledge.
12. A limited subject is called the ***topic***.
13. The point of view that you bring to your writing is called your ***worldview***.
14. The attitude that you bring to your writing is called ***tone***.
15. The most basic means of gathering raw material for your topic is through ***observation***.
16. Name three ways in which you may generate specific details to support your topic:
    a. ***Brainstorming***
    b. ***Grouping ideas or clustering***
    c. ***Answering the five "W's" and the "H"***
17. Raw material may be classified in what four ways?
    a. ***By searching for common elements***
    b. ***By categorizing according to importance***
    c. ***By using subdivisions of the main ideas***
    d. ***By discarding "misfit" items***
18. What are the five questions that must be answered during the *thinking process*?
    a. ***What is my goal in writing?***
    b. ***Who is my audience?***
    c. ***What is my topic?***
    d. ***What is my stance toward the topic?***
    e. ***How am I going to support my topic?***

19. A paragraph is defined as the ***rounded development*** of the main idea.
20. Name the four parts of an effective paragraph.
    a. ***Main idea*** c. ***Body of the paragraph***
    b. ***Topic sentence*** d. ***Summarizing sentence***
21. The ***main idea*** is the conscious determination of the writer to make every part of his writing move in *one* direction and conform to *one* clear intention.
22. A topic ***statement*** is an expression or mental construction of the main idea.
23. The ***topic*** sentence creates *unity* within the paragraph because it expresses the central thought among the sentences of the paragraph.
24. ***Supporting*** sentences develop or expand the main idea of the paragraph.
25. The ***summarizing (or concluding)*** sentence rounds off the discussion of the paragraph's topic, giving the reader a sense of completeness and closure.
26. List the nine ways in which a paragraph's topic may be developed. (*Order may vary.*)
    a. ***Examples and illustrations*** d. ***Chronology or sequence*** g. ***Definition***
    b. ***Particulars and details*** e. ***Contrast and comparison*** h. ***Reasons***
    c. ***Incident*** f. ***Causes and effects*** i. ***Division***
27. What is meant by *paragraph unity*? What is one thing unity does *not* mean?
    Paragraph unity is "oneness," when all the elements of a paragraph are relevant to the central thought of the topic. The one thing unity does not mean is "sameness."
28. Name three main kinds of progression that show orderly sentence arrangement in a paragraph.
    a. ***Time (chronological) order*** c. ***Logical order***
    b. ***Space (spatial) order***
29. Explain the difference between *inductive* and *deductive* logical order.
    The difference between inductive and deductive logical order is that, in inductive order, the writer first states particular points and then draws a general conclusion from them. In deductive order, the writer makes a general statement and then draws particular conclusions or individual truths from that general statement.
30. Normally, what is the most effective position for the most important sentence in a paragraph?
    The most effective position for the most important sentence in a paragraph is at the beginning or end of the paragraph.
31. What is meant by *proportion* in paragraph and composition writing?
    Proportion means that the ideas within a paragraph are developed according to their relative importance and that paragraphs are written with careful attention to how they relate to one another and to the composition as a whole.
32. What is meant by the term *transition* in paragraph and composition writing?
    Transition means passage from one place, condition, stage of development, type, or period of time to another. It applies to material which leads the reader from one idea or unit of composition to another.
33. What are the two kinds of resources that the writer needs to control?
    a. ***Personal resources*** b. ***Public resources***

34. What are the five steps in writing a composition?

a. *Writing the first draft*

b. *Appraising the first draft*

c. *Writing the second draft*

d. *Proofreading the second draft*

e. *Writing the final draft*

Unit 2 Writing a Research Paper

Teacher: These requirements are for students enrolled in the CLASS Administration Plan. They also may be useful to others as guidelines when completing their research paper.

Required Source Material[2]

- The "Works Cited" page must contain at least four sources, including two hard copy books or periodicals, or journals. (*Only one of the four sources may be an encyclopedia.*)
- If a survey or an experiment has been done, a table of collected data must be included.

Required Copies of Source Material

- Printouts of Internet articles or Web pages cited must be included.
- Photocopies of pages from articles and books that have been cited also need to be submitted. (*Include only pages that have been* ***cited in the paper****, not entire articles or whole sections from books.*)
- Words that have been quoted or ideas otherwise cited need to be **highlighted** in these copies.

Required Research Components

- Thesis statement (*The problem, possible approaches or solutions, and the writer's proposed approach must be expressed in this statement.*)
- Detailed outline (*It must contain three main sections: the introduction, the body, and the conclusion.*)
- Final draft of 1,500 words, double-spaced and typed on white paper
- "Works Cited" page (*It must contain at least four sources. See "Required Source Material" above.*)

Note: The student should also provide his teacher with the following components: *explanation of topic chosen, research plan, preliminary bibliography, thesis statement, outline, rough draft,* as well as the *final draft.*

LESSON 12: WHAT IS A RESEARCH PAPER?

✎ EXERCISE A (Page 39)

Answers will vary.

✎ EXERCISE B (Page 40)

The student needs to familiarize himself with the MLA style of documentation.

LESSON 13: WHERE DO I BEGIN?

✎ EXERCISE (Page 42)

The student needs to copy the eight-week plan (found on page 42) and write down a projected date when each step of the process will be completed.

---

2. Study "What Parents Should Know about Plagiarism" on pages vii and viii of this manual. For more advice, read Robert A. Harris's Web article entitled "FREE Anti-Plagiarism Tips" (visit <http://www.antiplagiarism.com/generic7.html>). Harris is the author of *The Plagiarism Handbook: Strategies for Preventing, Detecting, and Dealing with Plagiarism* (2001) and *Using Sources Effectively: Strengthening Your Writing and Avoiding Plagiarism* (2002).

LESSON 14: SELECTING AND LIMITING YOUR TOPIC

Teacher: The following section from *Writing a Research Paper* outlines for the student how to select a topic.

SELECT YOUR TOPIC

Now we are ready to take a closer look at each of the twelve steps for writing a research paper. Step one involves ***selecting*** and ***limiting your topic***. If you have not been assigned a general topic, you should choose one in which you are interested. Make sure you have sufficient resource material available, and then begin to limit your topic. By forming a workable topic, you will be able to adequately treat it within the specified number of pages.

A word needs to be said about the meaning of two often misunderstood words—subject and topic. These do not mean the same thing. A *subject* is a general, broad area of knowledge like "computers" or "politics." A *topic*, on the other hand, is a limited subject such as "the use of computers in the workplace" or "the influence of George Washington on the presidency." Consequently, this step deals with selecting a topic and then limiting it so it will become a *workable topic*.

❑ Selecting a Topic

What should you do if no topic has been assigned and you have to select your own? The best place to begin is with a topic that interests you or one in which you want to become an authority. No matter how interested you are in a topic, though, do not pursue one that has little source material available.

Generating Topic Ideas

Another place to gather topic ideas is from your local library. Scan through subjects in the card or computer catalog, articles in current periodicals, newspaper headlines, and items in the vertical file. The *Reader's Guide to Periodical Literature* and other reference works can also be a great source for topics. On-line Public Access Catalogs (OPACs) through your local library can be used as another way to generate ideas. You may use the World Wide Web and search various ideas which also may lead to a workable topic for your research paper.

Non-library sources for ideas are closer to home than you might think. If you belong to a home school network or you are in contact with other students at your school, meet together and discuss possible topic ideas. If you keep a writer's journal where you are constantly writing down thoughts and ideas, you could look over items you have recorded which might capture your imagination. Finally, brainstorming or clustering ideas on paper can go a long way in helping you pick the right topic for your work.

Avoiding Pitfalls

As you sift through various topic ideas, you need to avoid some pitfalls along the way. First, you are not writing an argumentative paper so avoid controversial topics about which you cannot be objective. Perhaps there may be a persuasive element in your writing, but your goal is exposition.

Second, some students think that the sole aim of a research paper is to write an encyclopedia-like composition. *This pitfall must also be avoided.* A research paper goes beyond mere definition or explanation. It should analyze the data gathered from various sources and reach a conclusion on an issue or problem that has been raised in the thesis statement.

Finally, avoid writing a biography. This involves extensive research of primary sources (correspondence, writings, interviews, etc.) which have not been published. You may, however, choose to write about a unique perspective or unusual aspect of a well-known figure.

❑ Limiting a Topic

In order to limit your topic, you need to get a basic overview of your subject material. The encyclopedia is a great place to begin your library reading. Skim through books as well to see how various authors approach your topic. This will help you not only begin to limit your topic but also to determine issues or questions to be addressed during the research process. Later, as you begin your serious reading and note taking, you will be able to focus your efforts in the right direction.

The Limiting Process

A topic cannot be stated in a few words or a short phrase. If you have written a topic that is less than five words, it is most likely too broad. You need to limit your topic by being specific. For example, you may be interested in "electronics" so you choose the general *subject* of "the electronics industry." Since this is very broad, you decide to discuss various electronic applications such as radar, X-ray machines, computers, etc. The more information you gather, however, you realize that your subject needs to be limited more. You decide to focus on "computers."

"Computers" is a broad subject in its own right; therefore, you need to limit your idea before it will be considered a topic. You are not interested in mainframes or minicomputers, so you choose microcomputers. This is still too large of a subject. Since you may not be able to contribute much to the technical aspects of computer design or manufacturing, you could learn more about the use of personal computers in the home. This becomes your limited subject—that is, your *topic*.

As you stop to consider your choice, you realize that this is still too large to be covered in your paper. You need to narrow it further. Since your topic should be more focused, you need to think about what you want to say about home computers. You settle on the limited topic of "the positive or negative impact computers have on home-users."

The following chart shows the process of limiting a topic for a research paper:

Procedures	Results
1. Select an area of interest	Electronics
2. Gain an overview of your subject	The electronics industry
3. Focus on one aspect of your subject	Computers
4. Choose a general topic	Home computers
5. Limit your topic	Impact on home-users

Clarifying Your Topic

The best way to state your limited topic is in the form of a sentence or thesis statement. This exercise will help you to clarify your thoughts. It will also help you focus on your topic as you begin your in-depth research. For example, "The impact of computers on home-users" might be stated as follows: "Home computers have impacted families for better or worse." Note that the noun *impact* in the phrase above has been changed into an action verb *impacted* in the sentence. Now you have a topic that is both interesting and promising. Writing your limited topic in the form of a thesis statement will be covered more under Step Three.

✎ **EXERCISE (Page 44)**

The student needs to write down the five questions of the ***thinking process*** *and begin to answer the first three questions. Answers will vary.*

Teacher: The following "answers" to the first three questions of the *thinking process* are only given as guidelines.

Question #1: The **goal** of a research paper is obvious—*expository.*

Question #2: The **topic** of the student's paper may not be finalized yet, but the ***subject*** matter should be chosen.

Question #3: The student should also begin to consider how his **stance** toward the topic will impact his thinking and writing.

LESSON 15: INITIAL LIBRARY RESEARCH

✎ **EXERCISE (Page 46)**

*The student needs to do his **initial library research**, evaluating sources and writing bibliography cards corresponding to each possible source. A functional "Works Cited" page should also be created.*

Teacher: The following section from *Writing a Research Paper* outlines for the student how to use the library.

The library enables you to access nearly any type and amount of information available in the English language, and more. In your desire to improve your research skills, the library stands out as one of the best resources. It not only has a fixed set of volumes, but may provide inter-library loan services and access to the Internet.

Upon entering the library, you should first ask someone at the front desk to help you get acquainted with your particular facility. The librarian is a specialist in the area of library science and can be an immense help in your library research. If the librarian is not available, look specifically for the card catalog.

THE "CARD CATALOG"

The card catalog has been traditionally housed in a large file-type cabinet, listing all the books available at your particular facility. Today, however, nearly all libraries have replaced the old card catalog system of accessing information with the computer terminal, which prompts you through a series of "commands" to help you locate the information you desire. In either case, there are three basic ways to locate a specific listing—by title, author, or subject. If it is a *fiction* book, then search for it by title or author; but if it is a *non-fiction* book, then look it up by title, author, or subject. All of these titles, authors, and subjects are listed in alphabetical order in the card or computer catalog.

❑ Dewey Decimal System

If your topic deals with the works of Charles Dickens, simply look under "D" or the name "Dickens" in the card catalog; or, if you want to increase your knowledge on insects, look under "Insects." You will be able to access the books listed by the ***call number*** or "Dewey decimal number" located in the upper left-hand corner of the cards in the card catalog.

If you are using the computer catalog, the number may be listed on the screen either to the right of the entries, if several truncated listings are given at once, or to the left as it would appear on a physical catalog card. If a printer is available, you do not need to write anything down—simply hit "p" for a printout of the items you want to locate. The electronic card catalog will even tell you if the book you want has been checked out and when it will be available.

Call numbers were devised by Melvil Dewey, who was a famous librarian and educator. Dewey is best known for originating the decimal system for classifying library books. The **Dewey Decimal System** is based on three-digit numbers—as shown below. These numbers are further extended beyond the decimal point for the various subclasses of books. Normally the library is divided up into sections according to these subjects. With the call number in hand, you will be able to find the section in the library stacks marked as follows:

THE DEWEY DECIMAL SYSTEM			
000–099	General Reference Works	500–599	Science
100–199	Philosophy	600–699	Technology
200–299	Religion	700–799	Arts & Recreation
300–399	Social Sciences	800–899	Literature
400–499	Language Arts	900–999	History

Each of these major headings are then divided further into sub-levels for more limited subjects, and then subdivisions for specific categories under each subject. These classifications are basically for non-fiction type books; however, all fiction books are listed under "Literature" in the Dewey Decimal System in alphabetical order by the last name of the author.

❑ Library of Congress System

The Library of Congress—which is considered one of the largest libraries in the world—offers an alternate classification system based on letters, rather than numbers, for major subjects. Although this system has greater flexibility than the Dewey Decimal System, it is more complex and lacks the logical decimal features of Dewey's system. The **Library of Congress system** is more suitable for larger libraries in academic and research fields. The general classifications for this system are given below:

A	General Works	N	Fine Arts
B	Philosophy, Psychology, Religion	P	Language & Literature
C	Auxiliary Sciences of History	Q	Science
D	History: General & Old World	R	Medicine
E-F	History: America	S	Agriculture
G	Geography, Anthropology, Recreation	N	Fine Arts
H	Social Sciences	T	Technology
J	Political Science	U	Military Science
K	Law	V	Naval Science
L	Education	Z	Library Science

REFERENCE BOOKS AND RESOURCES

Besides the books that you are able to check out and take home, there are many reference books that cannot be removed but may be very beneficial to your research objectives. The *encyclopedia* is the logical place to start for a general overview of any given subject. This resource provides summary articles, outlines, and sometimes a selected bibliography at the end of the entry. Please note that encyclopedias are used for subject overviews; at most, only one should be cited.

Other general reference works like dictionaries, thesauri, atlases, handbooks, almanacs, concordances, and indexes are useful for specific facts and support material in a given area. If you desire a more in-depth look, however, find reference books that contain detailed information on your topic. Keep in mind, though, that reference sources such as encyclopedias, dictionaries, etc. should rarely be cited in your paper as sources, unless they provide technical definitions or pertinent statistics that uniquely support your topic.

Not only should you utilize these reference works, but also magazine and newspaper articles, pamphlets, brochures, government documents, anthologies (collections of poems, stories, excerpts, etc.—chosen by a compiler), as well as non-print (microfilm, film, video, CD-ROM, DVD, and Internet) resources. These are just a portion of the holdings found in the reference section of your local library.

REFERENCE INDEXES AND GUIDES

The best approach to any kind of library research is reviewing a wide variety of sources. "But how can I find such a range of reference material on my particular topic?" you might ask. Besides the card catalog, there are several kinds of ***indexes*** available to you: newspaper and periodical indexes, vertical files (which hold pamphlets, brochures, etc., too small for the stacks), and the *Monthly Catalog of United States Documents*.

The most useful is *The Reader's Guide to Periodical Literature*, which lists published articles from about 170 of the most popular magazines in Canada and the United States. The most recent articles, essays, poems, speeches, and stories will help in giving you up-to-date information on your topic. The *Reader's Guide* is published twice a month, except for the months of February, July, and August when it is issued once; all entries are listed by author and subject—except stories, which are listed by title. This information is also available on CD-ROM and other electronic databases.

The *International Index* is similar, but covers over 250 American and foreign magazines that are more academically oriented. The *Essay and General Literature Index* is also a useful reference tool in locating articles, essays, and speeches found in collected works or compilations.

Another often overlooked resource is *The Encyclopedia of Associations*, which gives any particular organization's historian by name and lists certain specialists in your area of interest. If these experts live close by, you could make a point of interviewing them personally. If this is not possible, you could write, e-mail, or call them to gain valuable information you would not be able to get any other way.

Here are a few easy steps to follow when doing library research:

- ➢ Start with a general topic and outline, so you can focus your research and formulate a workable topic.
- ➢ Familiarize yourself with your local library.
- ➢ Get to know your librarian, who can help you find the resources you need.
- ➢ Then, go to the dictionary to look up any key words in your topic so you have a clear idea of what they mean.
- ➢ Next, refer to one of the primary encyclopedias such as *Britannica, Americana, Grolier's*, or *World Book*. This will give you an overview and historical background on the general topic you are researching.
- ➢ Do your initial research through various library and Internet resources.
- ➢ Consult the *Reader's Guide, Essay Index*, and other principal directories and indexes for more specific information.
- ➢ Another valuable resource tool is *The Basic Guide to Research Sources*, which lists government and private works, in all areas of knowledge.
- ➢ Make frequent use of your local library—one of your best resources for doing research.

The following brief listing gives various types of reference works that might be helpful for your research paper:

General Dictionaries

Oxford English Dictionary
Webster's Third New International Dictionary
The Random House Dictionary of the English Language

General Encyclopedias

Encyclopedia Britannica
Grolier's Encyclopedia
World Book Encyclopedia

Periodical Indexes

Reader's Guide to Periodical Literature
Humanities Index
Social Sciences Index
Ulrich's International Periodicals Directory

Bibliography Indexes

Bibliographic Index: A Cumulative Bibliography of Bibliographies
Library of Congress Catalog: Books, Subjects
The New York Times Guide to Reference Materials
A World Bibliography of Bibliographies

General Biography Indexes

Biography Index

Dictionary of American Biography

The New Century Cyclopedia of Names (three volumes)

Who's Who in America

Writers' Biography References

American Writers

Dictionary of Literary Biography

Twentieth Century Authors

The Writer's Directory

Almanacs and Yearbooks

Information Please Almanac

The International Yearbook & Statesmen's Who's Who

Whittaker's Almanac

World Almanac and Book of Facts

Atlases

The American Heritage Pictorial Atlas of United States History

The Canada Gazetteer Atlas

National Geographic Atlas of the World

Rand McNally Atlas of World History

Literature References

Bartlett's Familiar Quotations

Benét's *The Reader's Encyclopedia*

Granger's Index to Poetry

H. L. Mencken's *New Dictionary of Quotations*

Government Resources

Statutes of Canada

Congressional Record

Monthly Catalog of the United States Government Publications

Public Affairs Information Service Bulletin

Public Papers of the Presidents of the United States

LESSON 16: FOCUS YOUR THOUGHTS

✎ EXERCISE A (Page 47)

The student needs to write out an initial ***thesis statement****.*

✎ EXERCISE B (Page 47)

The student needs to write out his limiting questions.

✎ EXERCISE C (Page 48)

The student needs to determine his audience and the type of language and content he will use.

LESSON 17: PREPARE A GENERAL OUTLINE

✎ EXERCISE (Page 51)

The student needs to craft a ***general outline****, using the eight rules listed on page 49.*

LESSON 18: IN-DEPTH RESEARCH

✎ **EXERCISE A (Page 53)**

The student needs to become familiar with the source material that he has selected. He should begin to carefully read each source, marking promising passages for taking notes.

Teacher: Students should not write or mark in books that they do not own. They may use Post-it® notes.

✎ **EXERCISE B (Page 53)**

The student should carefully read each source and start taking notes.

LESSON 19: PREPARE A DETAILED OUTLINE

✎ **EXERCISE (Page 54)**

The student needs to prepare a detailed outline.

LESSON 20: WRITE YOUR FIRST DRAFT

✎ **EXERCISE (Page 54)**

The student needs to organize his note cards according to his detailed outline and to begin writing.

LESSON 21: DO ADDITIONAL RESEARCH

✎ **EXERCISE (Page 54)**

The student needs to examine what he has written in light of his thesis statement, limiting questions, audience, and detailed outline. If necessary, ***additional research*** *should be done at this time.*

LESSON 22: EDIT THE FIRST DRAFT AND WRITE THE SECOND

✎ **EXERCISE (Page 55)**

The student needs to go over his paper to improve its flow, to edit and rewrite the paper, and to proofread his work.

LESSON 23: TYPING YOUR FINAL DRAFT

✎ **EXERCISE A (Page 57)**

The student needs to type his paper according to the MLA guidelines. This may take several days.

✎ **EXERCISE B (Page 62)**

The student needs to prepare his bibliographical information and type his "Works Cited" page, following the MLA style.

LESSON 24: PROOFREAD YOUR PAPER

✎ **EXERCISE (Page 63)**

The student needs to proofread his paper carefully.

LESSON 25: PRODUCE THE FINAL DRAFT

✎ **EXERCISE (Page 63)**

The student needs to make any necessary changes or corrections, type the final copy, and submit it.

Teacher: A sample research paper is given so your student has an example of what is expected for this assignment. Note that a *thesis statement, detailed outline, the paper itself,* and a *"Works Cited" page* are required. Also, consult page 6 of this manual for other requirements that are essential.

Unit 3 Writing an Article of Opinion

LESSON 26: THE ARTICLE OF OPINION

✎ **EXERCISE (Page 76)**

The student needs to select three editorials from newspapers or magazines and analyze how the authors defend their opinions. Answers will vary.

Teacher: The four stages of argumentation that the student needs to mark are as follows: (1) the *opening stage*—the approach (*persuasion*) is clarified and the "rules of argumentation" are posited; (2) the *confrontation stage*—the debatable issue is explained; (3) the *argumentation stage*—reasons and evidence that support the opinion and prove the argument are given; and (4) the *closing stage*—the goal is achieved.

LESSON 27: SOUNDNESS OF ARGUMENT—PART 1

✎ **EXERCISE A (Page 77)**

The following exercise involves the debatable issue that **the movies need reform.**

	Issues Stated in the Form of Questions	*Relevant*	*Irrelevant*	*Combine*
1.	Do the movies need reform?	✔		
2.	Has censorship succeeded or failed in the past?		✔	
3.	Will censorship impair the artistic quality of the movies?	✔		✔
4.	Will censorship spoil their entertainment value?	✔		
5.	Will it curtail movie admissions and thus harm business?		✔	
6.	Who will do the censoring?	✔		
7.	How will Hollywood react?		✔	
8.	Why don't the movie studios censor themselves?	✔		
9.	Doesn't the public prefer uncensored pictures?		✔	
10.	Is censorship practical?	✔		✔
11.	Is censorship legal?	✔		
12.	Will it result in social good to the people as a whole?	✔		
13.	Why not wait and see what will happen?		✔	
14.	Will it increase taxes?		✔	

Teacher: The *four main issues which form the basis of the argument* are as follows: (1) the movies need reform; (2) censorship is a practical means of reform; (2) it will not harm the artistic quality of movies; and (4) it will result in the social good.

✎ EXERCISE B (Page 78)

1. *P* The study of art is more interesting than learning about computers.
2. *O* The government should not fund euthanasia through any entitlement programs.
3. *F* Homosexuality is condemned in the Bible as sexually deviant behavior.
4. *F* States' Rights was a key factor in the South ceding from the Union.
5. *O* The school year should follow a four-month pattern—three months of study and one month off—repeating the pattern to cover the twelve months of the year.
6. *F* Most doctors in Europe integrate both traditional and alternative medicine, whereas most doctors in the United States still frown upon alternative medical practices.
7. *F* By the age of twenty-six, Tiger Woods had won forty-three tournaments, thirty-one of which were achieved on the PGA Tour.
8. *O* Money spent on entitlements should be used for what government was designed to do—to uphold the Constitution, to maintain civil order, to defend the nation, etc.
9. *O* The Department of Education should be abolished because the federal government has gained excessive control over these state institutions.
10. *P* More students are preferring soccer—i.e., international "football"—over American football since the U.S. team placed in the World Cup.
11. *P* Traveling in the Middle East is more adventuresome than driving in the Indy 500.
12. *O* Followers of Christ should learn to defend their beliefs in the secular arena.
13. *F* C. S. Lewis was one of the most lucid Christian writers of the last century.
14. *O* Christian students should attempt to emulate Lewis's engaging writing style.
15. *F* The dictionary is a "friend" that you should keep close by whenever you write.

✎ EXERCISES C and D (Pages 79, 80)

Answers will vary.

LESSON 28: SOUNDNESS OF ARGUMENT—PART 2

✎ EXERCISE A (Page 82)

Teacher: The student needs to determine if the *evidence* listed in the chart below relates ***directly*** or ***indirectly*** to the issues surrounding the following *proposition* (thesis statement).

☞ **PROPOSITION:**

War inevitably devastates the lives of children, but not a single child should be engaged in the fighting. Children who become combatants before they gain emotional maturity suffer physically, mentally, and emotionally from military life and the horrors of war.

	Evidence Related to the Issues Surrounding the Proposition	*Directly*	*Indirectly*
1.	Casualty rates among child soldiers are generally high because of their lack of training.	✔	
2.	More than 300,000 children under the age of 18 are fighting in conflicts around the world.		✔

	Evidence Related to the Issues Surrounding the Proposition	*Directly*	*Indirectly*
3.	Many children have felt they had no choice but to "volunteer" for armed service; others have joined up voluntarily.		✔
4.	Due to inexperience, many child soldiers have died in action.	✔	
5.	Most of the children fighting with rebel forces in Sierra Leone have been abducted from their homes and families and forced to fight.	✔	
6.	Child soldiers have lower recovery rates from battlefield injuries than adult soldiers.		✔
7.	An Ethiopian high school student disclosed, "Everyone was dying. You saw the legs or hands of your friends lying in front of you. It was so horrifying, you couldn't make sense of it. It was hell!"	✔	
8.	Child soldiers are considered as especially useful because their size and agility means that they may be sent on hazardous assignments.		✔
9.	Many girl soldiers are expected to provide sexual services as well as fight.	✔	
10.	Peter, a 12-year-old, said: "When I was killing, I felt like it wasn't me doing these things. I had to because the rebels threatened to kill me."	✔	
11.	The majority of Afghan children have been witness to acts of violence and destruction which have destroyed the social fabric of their society.	✔	
12.	Children suffer more than adults from the rigors of military life, especially in the bush, and are particularly vulnerable to disease and malnutrition.	✔	
13.	To cope with combat, many former child soldiers with rebel forces were forced to drink alcohol and take drugs, or be beaten or killed.	✔	
14.	Young Ethiopian recruits tell harrowing stories of being marched over minefields to clear a path for the regular army.		✔

✎ EXERCISE B (Page 83)

Answers may vary.

Teacher: Using the same proposition, the student needs to review the following *evidence* and determine if it is ***trustworthy, fair,*** and ***current***. If the student does not know how to respond, he may leave the box blank.

	Evaluate the following statements based on Exercise A.	*Trustworthy*	*Fair*	*Current*
1.	Amnesty International calls for the end of child soldiery.	✔	✔	✔
2.	Tens of thousands of children partake in armed conflicts.	✔	✔	✘
3.	Children who join voluntarily should be allowed to fight.	✘	✘	✔
4.	Young girls are often exploited when inducted into the army.	✔	✔	✔
5.	Children suffer more than adults from the rigors of military life.	✔	✔	✔
6.	Child combatants were forced to take drugs for the fun of it.	✘	✘	✘
7.	Child soldiers suffer physically, emotionally, and mentally.	✔	✔	✔
8.	Most Afghan children have witnessed acts of violence.	✔	✔	✔
9.	Young Ethiopian recruits cleared minefields for regular army.	✔	✔	✘
10.	Child soldiers recover faster from battlefield injuries.	✘	✘	✘
11.	Many children have been forcibly recruited into rebel armies.	✔	✔	✔
12.	Due to inexperience, many child soldiers have died in action.	✔	✔	✔

✎ EXERCISE C (Page 84)

Answers will vary.

Teacher: The student needs to analyze three *articles of opinion* from magazines or journals to find out how the authors defended their opinions. A short paragraph is required for each article, verifying if the *evidence* meets the requirements as designated in the following three questions.

1. How does the evidence relate *directly* to the issues?
2. Why is the evidence *trustworthy, fair,* and *current*?
3. How does the evidence *defend the argument effectively*?

LESSON 29: SOUNDNESS OF ARGUMENT—PART 3

Teacher: Due to the amount of material covered in this lesson, it may be completed over several days. Each exercise would be a natural stopping point for each day's work.

✎ EXERCISE A (Page 85)

Answers will vary.

Teacher: The student needs to write a short paragraph about how each author used ***statistics*** to support his argument. Any weaknesses in the use of the statistics should be mentioned. The student is also required to include each author's *thesis statement* and determine if its *generalization* is upheld or not by the statistics.

✎ EXERCISE B (Page 88)

Answers will vary.

Teacher: The student needs to write a short paragraph about how each author used ***analogy*** to support his argument. The student should determine if the *analogies* are "logically sound" or not and the *parallels* are "plausible" or not. He is also required to include each author's *thesis statement* and determine if its *generalization* is upheld or not by the analogies or parallels.

✎ EXERCISE C (Page 91)

Teacher: The student needs to determine whether each *syllogism* is true or false. If the syllogism is false, he must explain why the particular syllogism is false.

	Syllogisms	*True*	*False*
1.	All two-legged creatures are human beings. An ostrich is a two-legged creature. An ostrich is a human being.		✔
	The major premise is false because there are many kinds of two-legged creatures besides human beings. Therefore, the conclusion is false even though the minor premise is true and the syllogistic formula was followed.		
2.	All people need love. Mary is a person. Mary needs love.	✔	
3.	Many seniors applied to college. Bill is a senior. Bill applied to college.		✔
	The major premise is false because "many" infers *some* but *not all* high school seniors applied. Therefore, the conclusion is false even though the minor premise is true and the syllogistic formula was followed. Bill may have applied, but not based on these premises.		

	Syllogisms	*True*	*False*
4.	Communists believe in state ownership of natural resources. Ruby believes in state ownership of oil reserves. Ruby is a communist.		✔
	Even though the major and minor premises are true, the conclusion is false because the major premise was taken as if *only* communists believe in state ownership of natural resources. This is a common fallacy of logic, which is covered next in this lesson.		
5.	All butterflies are insects. A monarch is a butterfly. A monarch is an insect.	✔	
6.	It is the duty of every American citizen eighteen and older to vote in every election. Renée is an eighteen-year-old American citizen. For this reason, it is Renée's duty to vote in every election.	✔	
7.	All birds have feathers. A gamin is a bird. A gamin has feathers.		✔
	Even though the major premise is true, the second premise is false; a *gamin* is a boy who hangs around on the streets, i.e., a street urchin. Therefore the conclusion is false.		
8.	The Denver Zephyr is the only nonstop train between Denver and Chicago. Cousin Fran, who lives just outside Denver, said she was coming to visit us via a nonstop train, so she must be traveling on the Zephyr.	✔	
9.	A gas-guzzler gets relatively few miles to the gallon. Since my van gets about fifteen miles to the gallon, it must be a gas-guzzler.		✔
	Even though the major premise is true, the second premise is false; *fifteen miles to the gallon* is not necessarily an indication that the van is a gas-guzzler. Thus the conclusion is false.		
10.	The cost for educating public high school students is greater than elementary students. Since more students will be attending high school in the future, the cost of public education will most certainly rise.		✔
	Even though the major and minor premises may be true; the conclusion may not. Two reasons why may be offered: (1) elementary enrollments may decrease to the point that costs will decrease; and (2) the future may offer cost-cutting means to public education.		

✎ **EXERCISE D (Page 93)**

Teacher: The student needs to identify what the fallacy is for each of the following *false arguments*.

	False Arguments	*Fallacy*
1.	Ann argued, "Mom, I should be allowed to wear make-up. All the other girls are."	***BW***
2.	The Republicans passed a tax rebate for all taxpayers; however, an economic downturn followed the passing of the new law. The Democrats claimed that the tax rebate caused the recession and they pushed to repeal it.	***FC***
3.	There is some merit in the Republicans' tax cut plan. Therefore, if Democrats are going to survive as a party, they should come up with something like it. They have got to be as tough-minded as the Republicans, since that is what the public wants.	***NS***
4.	You must resolve that you can afford this Bose Wave® Radio/CD, or you will be choosing to do without music for a while.	***FD***
5.	If euthanasia was legal, then it would not be prohibited by the law.	***BQ***

	False Arguments	Fallacy
6.	You believe that abortion is morally wrong because you're a priest. Moreover, you are just a lackey to the Pope, so I can't believe what you say.	*AP*
7.	The vast majority of people in this country believe that abortion is a right of every woman. To suggest that it isn't in the face of so much evidence is ridiculous.	*BW*
8.	A communist must not be allowed to hold government office and, if discovered, will lose his job. Consequently, a communist will do anything to hide his secret and will be open to blackmail, so he cannot be allowed to hold government office.	*AC*
9.	Jay bought a new computer and it worked fine for months. He then installed a new software program. The next time he started up his computer, it froze up. Jay deduced that the program must have caused the problem.	*NS*
10.	The belief in God is universal. After all, everyone believes in God.	*BW*

✎ **EXERCISE E (Page 95)**

Answers will vary.

Teacher: The student is required to write a false argument that corresponds to each of the seven fallacies described in this section. These fallacies are common errors in logic to which some fall prey.

LESSON 30: PRESENTATION

✎ **EXERCISE A (Page 96)**

Answers will vary.

Teacher: The student is required to write a paragraph explaining how the author seeks to create a *spirit of inquiry* in his audience.

✎ **EXERCISE B (Page 97)**

Answers will vary.

Teacher: The student is required to write a paragraph explaining how each author seeks to create a *tone of conciliation* in his audience.

LESSON 31: THINK BEFORE YOU WRITE

✎ **EXERCISE (Page 99)**

Answers will vary.

Teacher: The student is required to write the five questions of the *thinking process* and begin to fill in the appropriate information before he starts the *writing process.*

LESSON 32: THE WRITING PROCESS

Teacher: Note that the assignments in this lesson (pages 100 through 102) have not been marked off; however, each student is required to complete each of the five steps in the *writing process* and write an ***article of opinion*** that is approximately 1,000 words—carefully following the instructions given in the text.

LESSON 33: UNIT REVIEW

✎ EXERCISE A (Page 103)

1. ***Composition*** refers chiefly to structural arrangement, organization, the putting of parts to make a whole.
2. ***Rhetoric*** refers to the skill or artifice used in making composition persuasive and effective.
3. One of the four basic writing goals is to *persuade* or *convince*, that is, ***argumentative*** writing.
4. This type of writing ***influences***, ***reasons***, or ***gives opinions***.
5. A(n) ***article of opinion*** is a formal essay that deals with a debatable issue in a serious and definitive manner.
6. List the four stages of *argumentative communication.*
   a. ***Opening stage***
   b. ***Confrontation stage***
   c. ***Argumentation stage***
   d. ***Closing stage***
7. What are the two questions at the heart of an *article of opinion*?
   What is a sound argument? ***How is a sound argument presented well?***
8. What three factors are the basis of a *sound argument*?
   a. ***Thesis statement or proposition***
   b. ***Evidences or solid, established facts***
   c. ***Rules of logic or laws of thought***
9. The conscious decision of the writer to make every part of his writing move in *one* direction and conform to *one* clear intention is called the ***main idea***.
10. In formal argumentation, a *thesis statement* is called the ***proposition***.
11. A *thesis statement* should be a ***debatable*** issue that allows reasoned *affirmative* and *negative* arguments.
12. A(n) ***opinion*** is an inference or conviction that can be debated, because it cannot be proved, or tested, like a *fact*.
13. A thesis statement, or *proposition*, may have words that are misunderstood, so these terms should be ***defined***.
14. A *proposition* needs to be ***precise***—that is, accurate in grasping and expressing the issues which are to be debated.
15. A proposition should have a ***plan*** of ***action***.
16. The issues surrounding your thesis statement need to rest upon conclusive ***evidence***.
17. What three requirements must the *evidence* you gather meet?
   a. ***Relate directly to the issues***
   b. ***Be trustworthy, fair, and current***
   c. ***Be presented so that it defends the argument effectively***
18. An article of opinion must have *evidence* that ***unifies*** the argument—that is, evidence that relates directly to the debatable issues.
19. After evidence has been gathered, you must determine if it is ***trustworthy***, ***fair***, and ***current***—that is, if it is *reliable evidence* or not.
20. If you are going to defend your argument effectively, you must offer ***enough*** evidence, so that your readers may conclude that your premises are *plausible* and *defensible*.
21. The amount of evidence that should be offered is a matter of ***judgment*** and ***proportion***.

22. How is a *sound argument* ordered?

    A sound argument is ordered by the laws of thought—in other words, the rules of logic.

23. *Sound logic* is emphasized by studying ***inductive*** and ***deductive*** reasoning.

24. Define the two types of reasoning mentioned in the previous question.

    In inductive reasoning, the writer first states particular points and then draws a general conclusion from them. In deductive reasoning, the writer makes a general statement and then draws particular conclusions or individual truths from that general statement.

25. *Logical* ***inference*** is made, based on the truth of the respective bits of evidence that have been presented.

26. ***Induction*** is the same logical process used in the *scientific method.*

27. The above inductive method may be approximated through *arguing by the use of* ***statistics*** and *arguing by* ***analogy***.

28. In ***deductive*** reasoning, a principle or assumption is established and then applied to a set of particulars.

29. A(n) ***syllogism*** is the form of an argument that has a *major premise*, a *minor premise*, and a *conclusion.*

30. The *major premise* states a ***generalization***; the *minor premise* states a ***particular***; and the *conclusion* draws a ***logical connection*** that is obvious between the major and minor premises.

31. The difference between *pure logic* and *persuasive writing* is that the main premise normally is not an axiom or theorem but an ***expressed opinion***.

32. Write the *syllogistic formula* below.

    If all A is C, and all B is A, then all B is C.

✎ EXERCISE B (Page 105)

Teacher: The student needs to identify what the fallacy is for each of the following *false arguments.*

	False Arguments	*Fallacy*
1.	Since I'm not lying, it follows that I'm telling the truth.	***AC***
2.	Polls suggest that the Liberals will form a majority government, so you may as well vote for them.	***BW***
3.	Smoking is not harmful. Why my grandmother smoked a pack a day and lived to the ripe old age of 92.	***FC***
4.	Either you're for me or against me.	***FD***
5.	The problem in this community is that it has no library.	***AC***
6.	You may argue that God does not exist, but you are just following a fad.	***BQ***
7.	The sign said "Fine For Parking Here," and since it was fine, I parked there.	***FC***
8.	Abortion should remain legal because it is every woman's right to have one.	***NS***
9.	**Reporter:** "Senator, what about these allegations of taking campaign money from the Chinese?" **Senator:** "I'm glad you asked me that. This bipartisan bill that I'm introducing will reform campaign finance in this country."	***RH***
10.	America: love it or leave it.	***FD***

✎ EXERCISE C (Page 105)

Teacher: The student is asked to match the following *fallacies* in the left column to the respective *false arguments* or *posturings* listed in the right column.

Fallacy	False Argument/Posturing
card stacking	Noted psychologist Dr. Frasier Crane recommends that you buy the EZ-Rest Hot Tub.
false analogy	Bill Clinton: "We want to build a bridge to the future. Bob Dole talks about building a bridge to the past."
false authority	The United States is a Christian nation; therefore, each American is Christian.
hasty generalization	A current events program has three liberal panelists, plus a like-minded host, while there is only one conservative guest.
slippery slope/ domino theory	If I make an exception for you then I have to make an exception for everyone.
straw man	Most Democrats promote liberal issues, so voters should not trust their candidates who claim to be pro-life.
sweeping generalization	Employees are like nails. Just as nails must be hit in the head in order to make them work, so must employees.

✎ EXERCISE D (Page 106)

1. The final step in the *thinking process* is the ***presentation*** of an article of opinion.
2. What *two elements* should this final step seek to cultivate?
   a. ***Spirit of inquiry***
   c. ***Tone of conciliation***
3. The facts presented in your article of opinion should lead your readers to further ***investigation***.
4. A(n) ***conciliatory*** *approach* produces a more positive response in your audience, if your argument is presented in a fair manner.
5. The best way to establish a *tone of conciliation* is to begin with a ***point of agreement***.
6. What are the five questions that need to be answered during the *thinking process*?
   a. ***What is my goal in writing?***
   b. ***Who is my audience?***
   c. ***What is my topic?***
   d. ***What is my stance toward the topic?***
   e. ***How am I going to support my topic?***
7. What are the five steps in writing a composition?
   a. ***Writing the first draft***
   b. ***Appraising the first draft***
   c. ***Writing the second draft***
   d. ***Proofreading the second draft***
   e. ***Writing the final draft***

✎ EXERCISE E (Page 106)

Answers will vary.

Teacher: The student needs to analyze the article of opinion on page 96 of the workbook. The author's *thesis statement, stance, audience,* and *evidence* must be covered. The soundness of the author's argument and his presentation must also be discussed.

Unit 4 The Mechanics of Good Writing

LESSON 34: PROPER NOUNS AND ADJECTIVES

✎ **EXERCISE (Page 110)**

1. the Islands of the south Pacific
2. the amazon river
3. an ethiopian village
4. nantahala national forest
5. the italian dolomites
6. DuPage county
7. the chicago expressways
8. the ancient Caspian sea
9. the great basin national park
10. the Nations of Southern Asia
11. the Seaside resort along the mediterranean
12. Village of Radium Hot Springs, BC, Canada
13. province of Prince Edward island
14. the alaskan oil reserves
15. shenandoah national park
16. 1061 e. main st., dundee, illinois
17. a Hotel on the gulf of mexico
18. irving park road runs east and west.
19. the angolan people
20. christmas island in the indian ocean

LESSON 35: GROUPS AND EVENTS

✎ **EXERCISE (Page 111)**

Answers will vary.

LESSON 36: OTHER PROPER NAMES

✎ **EXERCISE (Page 113)**

1. Tylenol may be less harmful to the stomach than Aspirin, but tylenol is bad for the Liver.
2. Completion of the Sophomore course called algebra II is required for advanced Mathematics.
3. Jesus christ is called the alpha and omega, the beginning and the end (revelation 1:8, nkjv).
4. It is no coincidence that intel chips are manufactured by intel corporation.
5. Officials from the state department in washington, d.c., visited several areas in the balkans.
6. Our gas and electricity come from the northern indiana public service company (nipsco).
7. No one from the earth has yet set foot on mars, but several men have been on the Moon.
8. His Grandfather, the famous theologian h. bavinck, taught him the heidelberg catechism.
9. Reverend john mitchell of yorkshire, England—a Geologist and Astronomer, as well as a clergyman—predicted the existence of Black Holes in 1784, using newtonian Physics.
10. Charles darwin's grandfather erasmus—physician, poet, philosopher, botanist, and naturalist—formulated a comparable Theory of Evolution some sixty years before charles had.

LESSON 37: TITLES AND OTHER CAPITALIZATION

✎ **EXERCISE (Page 114)**

Answers will vary.

Teacher: The next few lessons include practice exercises after each point within each lesson. After the student reads each example(s) given with each rule, he is to write a sentence to illustrate the rule.

LESSON 38: END PUNCTUATION

✎ **EXERCISE (Pages 115–116)**

Answers will vary.

LESSON 39: A CAUSE TO PAUSE

✎ **EXERCISE (Pages 116–124)**

Answers will vary.

LESSON 40: SIGNS ALONG THE WAY

✎ **EXERCISE (Pages 124–129)**

Answers will vary.

✎ **EXERCISE (Page 127)**

"Ultimately your children must internalize the message of the Gospel. Each child in a Christian home will at some point examine the claims of the Gospel and determine whether he will embrace the truth.

"Picture the process this way: he holds the claims of the Gospel at arm's length, turning it in the hand and determining either to embrace it or cast it away.

"The parent has the marvelous opportunity to help his young adult child pursue with honesty all his questions of faith. The Word of God is robust; Christian faith can withstand close, honest scrutiny. Everyone does not have the obligation to ask every question, but everyone has the obligation to ask every question he has.**"** [*Quote marks are in **bold**.*]

LESSON 41: INDENTATION AND ALTERNATIVES

✎ **EXERCISE (Page 132)**

Answers will vary.

LESSON 42: SPACING AND ALIGNMENT

✎ **EXERCISE (Page 133)**

Answers will vary.

LESSON 43: UNIT REVIEW

✎ **EXERCISE A (Page 133)**

On Wednesday ... *Chargers* ... *Christian High*

1. __X__ ~~on wednesday~~, our team, the ~~chargers~~, defeated the team from Bethel ~~christian high~~.

Mr. Kostelny ... *baseball*

2. __X__ ~~mr. kostelny~~, our history teacher, also coaches our ~~Baseball~~ team.

3. __C__ This fall, the freshman class will be the largest in the history of our school.

Institute ... *The Asheville Citizen-Times*

4. __X__ The World Journalism ~~institute~~ has a working agreement with ~~the asheville citizen-times~~.

Frost's ***Death*** ***Hired***
5. _X_ ~~frost's~~ importance as a poet derives from "The ~~death~~ of the ~~hired~~ Man" and other poems.

6. _C_ WORLD magazine always tries to publish articles with a Christian worldview.

religion ***Middle East***
7. _X_ The Islamic ~~Religion~~ has inspired violence in some countries of the ~~middle east~~.

English
8. _X_ My great aunt wanted to learn ~~english~~, but Grandpa George insisted she could not.

Hudson Bay ***beluga***
9. _X_ The ~~hudson bay~~ area is known as a sanctuary for ~~Beluga~~ whales.

Reconstruction ***Republic*** ***I*** ***Arlington Public Library***
10. _X_ The ~~reconstruction~~ *of the* ~~republic~~ was the last book ~~i~~ checked out of ~~arlington public library~~.

11. _C_ He graduated from Elgin High School and then attended Covenant College.

president ***college*** ***East***
12. _X_ Jordan, ~~President~~ of our class, has won a scholarship to attend a prestigious ~~College~~ in the ~~east~~.

capital ***south*** ***Sea***
13. _X_ Jakarta, the ~~Capital~~ of Indonesia, is situated on the Island of Java, ~~South~~ of the Java ~~sea~~.

Island
14. _X_ Is there a Hilton Hotel on Hilton Head ~~island~~?

I ***Okay*** ***I'm***
15. _X_ ~~i~~ cannot find any errors in this sentence. ~~okay~~, ~~i'm~~ only joking!

✎ EXERCISE B (Page 134)

Two men, Saddam Husayn and Bakr, increasingly dominated the [Baath] party. Bakr, who had been associated with Arab nationalist causes for more than a decade, brought the party popular legitimacy. Even more important, he brought support from the army both among Baathist and non-Baathist officers_ with whom he had cultivated ties for years. Saddam Husayn, on the other hand, was a consummate party politician whose formative experiences were in organizing clandestine opposition activity. He was adept at outmaneuvering—and at times ruthlessly eliminating—political opponents. Although Bakr was the older and more prestigious of the two, by 1969 Saddam Husayn clearly had become the moving force behind the party. He personally directed Baathist attempts to settle the Kurdish question and he organized the party's institutional structure.

In July 1973, after an unsuccessful coup attempt by a civilian faction within the Baath led by Nazim Kazzar, the party set out to reconsolidate its hold on power. First, the RCC [Revolutionary Command Council] amended the Provisional Constitution to give the president greater power. Second, in early 1974 the Regional Command was officially designated as the body responsible for making policy. By September 1977, all Regional Command leaders had been appointed to the RCC. Third, the party created a more pervasive presence in Iraqi society by establishing a complex network of grass_roots and intelligence-gathering organizations. Finally, the party established its own militia, which in 1978 was reported to number close to 50,000 men.

Despite Baath attempts to institutionalize its rule, real power remained in the hands of a narrowly based elite, united by close family and tribal ties. By 1977 the most powerful men in the Baath thus were all somehow related to the triumvirate of Saddam Husayn, Bakr, and General Adnan

Khayr Allah Talfah, Saddam Husayn's brother-in-law who became minister of defense in 1978. All were members of the party, the RCC, and the cabinet; and all were members of the Talfah family of Tikrit, headed by Khayr Allah Talfah. Khayr Allah Talfah was Saddam Husayn's uncle and guardian, Adnan Khayr Allah's father, and Bakr's cousin. Saddam Husayn was married to Adnan Khayr Allah's sister and Adnan Khayr Allah was married to Bakr's daughter. Increasingly, the most sensitive military posts were going to the Tikritis.

Beginning in the mid-1970_s, Bakr was beset by illness and by a series of family tragedies. He increasingly turned over power to Saddam Husayn. By 1977 the party bureaus, the intelligence mechanisms, and even ministers who, according to the Provisional Constitution, should have reported to Bakr, reported to Saddam Husayn. Saddam Husayn, meanwhile, was less inclined to share power; and he viewed the cabinet and the RCC as rubber stamps. On July 16, 1979, President Bakr resigned; and Saddam Husayn officially replaced him_ as president of the republic, secretary general of the Baath Party Regional Command, chairman of the RCC, and commander in chief of the armed forces.

In foreign affairs, the Baath's pan-Arab and socialist leanings alienated both the pro-Western Arab Gulf states and the shah of Iran. The enmity between Iraq and Iran sharpened with the 1969 British announcement_ of a planned withdrawal from the Gulf in 1971. In February 1969, Iran announced that Iraq had not fulfilled its obligations under the 1937 treaty and demanded that the border in the Shatt al Arab waterway be set at the thalweg. Iraq's refusal to honor the Iranian demand led the shah to abrogate the 1937 treaty and to send Iranian ships through the Shatt al Arab without paying dues to Iraq. In response, Iraq aided anti-shah dissidents, while the shah renewed support for Kurdish rebels. Relations between the two countries soon deteriorated further. In November 1971, the shah occupied the islands of Abu Musa and the Greater and Lesser Tunbs, which previously had been under the sovereignty of Ras al Khaymah and Sharjah, both member states of the United Arab Emirates.

The Iraqi Baath also was involved in a confrontation_ with the conservative shaykhdoms of the Gulf over Iraq's support for the leftist People's Democratic Republic of Yemen (South Yemen) and the Popular Front for the Liberation of the Occupied Arabian Gulf. The major contention between Iraq and the conservative Gulf states, however, concerned the Kuwaiti islands of Bubiyan and Warbah that dominate the estuary leading to the southern Iraqi port of Umm Qasr. Beginning in the early 1970_s, Iraq's desire to develop a deepwater port on the Gulf led to demands that the two islands be transferred or leased to Iraq. Kuwait refused; and in March 1973 Iraqi troops occupied As Samitah, a border post in the northeast corner of Kuwait. Saudi Arabia immediately came to Kuwait's aid and, together with the Arab League, obtained Iraq's withdrawal.

The most serious threat facing the Baath was a resurgence of Kurdish unrest in the north. In March 1970, the RCC and Mustafa Barzani announced agreement to a fifteen-article peace plan. This plan was almost identical to the previous Bazzaz-Kurdish settlement that had never been implemented. The Kurds were immediately pacified by the settlement, particularly because Barzani was permitted to retain his 15,000 Kurdish troops. Barzani's troops then became an official Iraqi frontier force called the Pesh Merga, meaning "Those Who Face Death." The plan, however, was not completely satisfactory because the legal status of the Kurdish territory remained unresolved. At the time of the signing_ of the peace plan, Barzani's forces controlled territory from Zakhu in the north to Halabjah in the southeast and already had established de facto Kurdish administration in most of the towns of the area. Barzani's group, the Kurdish Democratic Party (KDP), was granted official recognition as the legitimate representative of the Kurdish people.

—From *Iraq: A Country Study*, edited by Helen Chapin Metz
Federal Research Division, Library of Congress, May 1988

EXERCISE C (Page 136)

1. *Indentation* is *the offsetting of the first line of a paragraph a specified distance to the right of the left margin.*
2. Describe the three types of indentation, including the two variations of the third style.
   a. *Standard paragraph indentation is about one-quarter of an inch, or it is measured by a measure known as an "em"—a space approximately equal to the width of the letter "M."*
   b. *In block style indentation, all lines begin at the left margin without indenting the first line; paragraphs are then distinguished by leaving a line of space between each paragraph.*
   c. *Hanging indentation is opposite of the standard indentation, for only the first line begins at the left margin, and all the following lines in the paragraph are indented.*
      1. *The numbered paragraph is a variation of the hanging indentation where a number or letter is placed at the beginning of the first line and at the left margin; the text of the first line and all subsequent lines are indented with a line of space inserted between each paragraph.*
      2. *The bulleted paragraph is another variation of the hanging indentation which is identical to the numbered paragraph except that a certain device or symbol known as a "bullet" or "dingbat" is used to mark each paragraph instead of a number or letter.*
3. Describe the two ways *spacing* is used in paragraphs.

   Traditionally, two spaces have been inserted between the end of one sentence and the beginning of the next; however, with advent of electronic typesetting, only one space is placed between sentences.
4. What is the preferred method of *alignment*? Why?

   The preferred method of alignment is where each line of text extends from the left margin to the right margin, unless the last line ends before reaching to the full extent of the line. This method is preferred because it avoids confusion and unnecessary eye movement on the part of the reader.
5. List various ways word processors and computers can align text.
   a. *Full justification aligns lines of words along a straight line on both the right and left margins.*
   b. *"Flush left" aligns text along a straight line only on the left margin and the right is "jagged."*
   c. *Center alignment is used not for paragraphs but for titles, headlines, and subheadings.*

EXERCISE D (Page 137)

Answers will vary.

Teacher: The student is required to describe in a couple of paragraphs how the author used good writing mechanics in the article provided. Any errors that are found should be included.

Unit 5 Colorful Writing

LESSON 44: SYNONYMS AND ANTONYMS

✎ **EXERCISE (Page 140)** *Answers will vary. Sample answers are given.*

	Synonyms		Antonyms
1. hostile	*antagonistic*	1. arrogant	*humble*
2. apparent	*evident*	2. harmful	*harmless*
3. ascend	*climb*	3. rough	*smooth*
4. difficult	*arduous*	4. huge	*bantam*
5. meager	*scant*	5. decrease	*increase*
6. arrogant	*pompous*	6. adequate	*insufficient*
7. joyous	*happy*	7. faithful	*faithless*
8. rebuke	*admonition*	8. talkative	*silent*
9. cordial	*gracious*	9. refined	*crude*
10. defame	*malign*	10. fruitful	*infertile*

LESSON 45: HOMONYMS AND HOMOGRAPHS

✎ **EXERCISE A (Page 141)**

Teacher: The student is asked to write *homonyms* for the following list of words.

1. peace	*piece*	11. their	*there, they're*
2. deer	*dear*	12. wrest	*rest*
3. would	*wood*	13. shear	*sheer*
4. herd	*heard*	14. sew	*so, sow*
5. know	*no*	15. whether	*weather*
6. rain	*reign*	16. stationary	*stationery*
7. who's	*whose*	17. shone	*shown*
8. new	*knew*	18. shutter	*shudder*
9. scent	*cent, sent*	19. led	*lead*
10. flue	*flu, flew*	20. passed	*past*

✎ **EXERCISE B (Page 141)**

Teacher: The student is asked to write definitions for the sets of *homonyms* or *near-homonyms.*

2. slay	*to kill violently, wantonly, or in great numbers; to strike down; kill*
sleigh	*an open, usually horse-drawn, vehicle with runners for use on snow or ice*
3. principle	*a comprehensive and fundamental law, doctrine, or assumption*
principal	*most important, consequential, or influential; chief*
4. course	*the act of moving in a path from point to point; the path over which something moves*
coarse	*of ordinary or inferior quality or value; loose or rough in texture; crude or unrefined*

5. counsel	*advice given especially as a result of consultation; deliberation, consultation*
council	*an assembly or meeting for consultation, advice, or discussion; legislative body*
consul	*an official appointed by a government to reside in a foreign country to represent the commercial interests of citizens of the appointing country; ambassador; envoy*
6. do	*to bring to pass; carry out;*
due	*owed or owing as a debt; owed or owing as a natural or moral right; adequate*
7. capital	*top of column; most important; seat of government; having to do with wealth*
capitol	*a building in which a state legislative body meets*
8. accept	*to receive willingly; to be able or designed to take or hold; believe*
except	*with the exclusion or exception of*

✎ **EXERCISE C (Page 142)**

Teacher: The student is asked to write definitions for the sets of *homographs*. NOTE: There may be other definitions or connotations assigned to these terms. Therefore, the ***answers may vary.***

1. row	*to propel a boat by means of oars*
row	*a number of objects arranged in a usually straight line; way, street*
row	*a noisy disturbance or quarrel; to engage in a row; have a quarrel*
2. air	*the mixture of invisible odorless tasteless gases that surrounds the earth; breeze*
air	*an accompanied song or melody in usually strophic form; tune, melody*
air	*outward appearance of a thing; a surrounding or pervading influence; "atmosphere"*
3. bow	*a weapon that is made of a strip of flexible material with a cord connecting the two ends and holding the strip bent and that is used to propel an arrow*
bow	*to bend the head, body, or knee in reverence, submission, shame, salutation, assent*
bow	*something bent into a simple curve; rainbow, bow window*
bow	*the forward part of a ship*
4. lead	*to guide on a way notably by going in advance; to direct on a course or in a direction*
lead	*a heavy, soft, malleable, bluish-gray metallic chemical element that is used especially in pipes, cable sheaths, batteries, solder, and shields against radioactivity*

LESSON 46: TROPES

✎ **EXERCISE A (Page 145)**

metonymy	1. The White House issued no public statement about the incident.
onomatopoeia	2. Just then, several skiers whooshed down the hill past me.
metaphor	3. Some modern thinkers are foolish sages indeed.
oxymoron	4. This lovely weed certainly has a fragrant stench.
litotes	5. She's not the friendliest person I know.
simile	6. Tommy yelped like a whipped puppy after his dad punished him.
antithesis	7. "Fair is foul and foul is fair" (*Shakespeare*).
personification	8. I heard dinner calling me to the table.
hyperbole	9. When he saw her costume, his jaw dropped to the floor.
alliteration	10. "What a tale of terror, now their turbulency tells!" (*Poe*)
synecdoche	11. "Give us this day our daily bread…"
apostrophe	12. "Rain, rain, go away, come again some other day."

✎ **EXERCISE B (Page 145)**

Answers will vary.

✎ **EXERCISE C (Page 146)** ***Answers will vary, but the synonym must convey a different connotation.***

1. funny *ridiculous*
2. naive *trusting*
3. wise *discerning*
4. arrogant *narcissistic*
5. cunning *shrewdness*
6. deliberate *premeditated*

LESSON 47: DIALOGUE

✎ **EXERCISE (Page 148)**

Dialogues will vary.

LESSON 48: PARAPHRASING

✎ **EXERCISE (Page 150)**

Paraphrases will vary.

LESSON 49: AMPLIFYING MEANING

✎ **EXERCISE (Page 151)**

Paragraphs will vary.

LESSON 50: DESCRIPTIVE WRITING

✎ **EXERCISE A (Page 154)** *Answers will vary.*

1. Nouns: *emporium, promontory, fetters, costume, creatures, refuse, siesta, flamingoes*
2. Verbs: *crowned, jars, defies, spinning, roam, reigns, devouring, wakes up, obtained, beat*

✎ **EXERCISE B (Page 154)**

Descriptive paragraphs will vary.

LESSON 51: SKETCHES

✎ **EXERCISE A (Page 157)**

Character sketches will vary.

✎ **EXERCISE B (Page 157)**

Type sketches will vary.

LESSON 52: UNIT REVIEW

✎ **EXERCISE A (Page 157)**

1. It is extremely important not to (altar, alter) the meaning of Scripture by paraphrasing.
2. The thane of Cawdor was greedy and wanted the (throne, thrown) of England for himself.
3. We will begin reading the play (hear, here), at the beginning of the second act.
4. A proverb is a statement of (principle, principal) more than a rule of law.
5. The heels of her feet were (course, coarse) due to the dry, winter weather.
6. My youth leader (cent, scent, sent) me a reminder about the Saturday mission project.
7. The company name was printed at the top of his business (stationery, stationary).

8. Our freedom has allowed us to forget that (their, there, they're) is a price to follow Christ.
9. To start a business of your own, you need an adequate amount of (capital, capitol).
10. In A.D. 155, Polycarp, the faithful elder of the church at Smyrna, was burned at the (steak, stake).

EXERCISE B (Page 157) ***Answers may vary.***

1. The birth of a baby is always a miraculous **event** in a family's life. ***milestone***
2. The **sense** of the cryptic message was hard to discern. ***meaning***
3. The **job** of building a coalition of nations to stop terrorism was immense. ***task***
4. You must follow the **rules** of the game if you wish to play. ***regulations***
5. The business **stores** inventory in various locations all over the county. ***warehouses***
6. The **main** event will be held in the Grand Ballroom of the Palmer House. ***primary***
7. He felt quite **fatigued** after his transplant surgery. ***debilitated***
8. A beluga whale **consumes** about 40 to 80 pounds of food a day. ***devours***
9. The young man **pursued** his dreams to the neglect of his family. ***followed***
10. The programers **developed** a database designed for their unique needs. ***formed***

EXERCISE C (Page 158)

1. A (dairy, diary) is a book used to record (personal, personnel) thoughts.
2. There is a (statue, statute, stature) of Stonewall Jackson on the grounds of the West Virginia State (Capitol, Capital) building.
3. Christians have formed many interpretations of the (prophecy, prophesy) of Daniel.
4. The Seventh Commandment requires (marital, martial) faithfulness.
5. San Diego's (climatic, climactic) conditions are often described as ideal.
6. The film director employed a variety of amazing special (affects, effects).
7. The movie was (all together, altogether) hilarious.
8. The Israelites wandered for forty years in the (deserts, desserts) of the Sinai Peninsula.
9. The fugitive was able to (allude, elude) the police for four days.
10. Chocolate syrup is the perfect (complement, compliment) for vanilla ice cream.
11. The children were (anxious, eager) to see their loving grandparents.
12. The climbers' (descent, decent) from the mountain was slow and treacherous.

EXERCISE D (Page 158)

1. The term *trope* means ***the use of a word or expression in a figurative way***.
2. *Denotation* is ***the literal, most ordinary, dictionary meaning of a word***.
3. *Connotation* is ***the meaning that is implied in, suggested by, or associated with a word***.
4. Give definitions or descriptions of the following figures of speech or literary devices:

   Synecdoche

   Synecdoche is a figure of speech in which a part of a thing represents the whole.

   Metonymy

   In metonymy, two different items are so closely related that they take on the characteristics of each other.

Oxymoron

Oxymoron is a combination or blending of two contradictory or inconsistent terms.

Antithesis

Antithesis is the more deliberate contrasting of two ideas or terms for the purpose of highlighting their differences.

Apostrophe

Apostrophe is an imaginary addressing of a person or thing that is absent or dead, or the addressing of an inanimate object as if it could hear or understand.

Hyperbole

Hyperbole is the use of gross exaggeration for the purpose of making a point.

Litotes

Litotes is the use of understatement to convey an opposite meaning or to increase an effect.

Simile

Simile is a comparison using "like" or "as."

Metaphor

Metaphor is an implied comparison without the use of "like" or "as."

Personification

Personification is the giving of human characteristics to objects, ideas, or animals.

Alliteration

Alliteration is the repetition of word sounds—particularly initial sounds.

Onomatopoeia

Onomatopoeia is the use of words whose pronunciation sounds like their meanings.

5. *Attribution* in dialogue is ***the identity of the person speaking.***
6. If a quotation is longer than one sentence, place quotation marks ***only at the beginning of the first sentence and the end of the last sentence.***
7. Paraphrasing is ***the rewording of a piece of writing***.
8. List three ways to add *meaning* to your writing.
   a. ***Using synonyms and antonyms***
   b. ***Providing the reader with the word's history***
   c. ***Using illustration, stories, and examples to show what the word means in the lives of real people***
9. In writing description, it is wise to use words that appeal to the five ***senses***.
10. The two kinds of sketches are ***character*** sketches and ***type*** sketches. What is the difference between these two?

    Character sketches are word portraits of specific individuals. They present information that sets off the person being described from others. They describe individual personality traits and physical or historical features of that particular person. A type sketch, however, does the opposite. It describes a general class of people, rather than an individual. This description has also been called a stereotype.

EXERCISE E (Page 160)

Answers will vary.

Teacher: The student is asked to identify the various elements that make Whyte's article a *character sketch.* The following information may be included in some form in the student's answer.

---

1. Choosing a Suitable Character

The author, Alexander Whyte, chose Samuel Rutherford[3] as the focus of his character sketch. Rutherford was famous in Scotland "as a scholar, a theologian, a controversialist, a preacher and a [true] saint." Whyte's choice was undoubtedly due to Rutherford's "talents, his industry, his scholarship, his preaching power, his pastoral solicitude and his saintly character."

2. Disclosing a General Impression

The general impression Whyte wishes to give his readers about Rutherford is accomplished through a comparison of Rutherford to Joshua—"Moses' spy and pioneer, Moses' successor and the captain of the Lord's covenanted host." To support this general impression, Whyte gives details regarding Rutherford's "character and ... services."

3. Selecting Details Carefully

Whyte supports his "Joshua Redivivus" as follows: As God chose Joshua as "the best and the ablest [man] he could lay hold," so God chose Rutherford. Whyte details Rutherford's talents and industry as a student at Edinburgh, his scholarship and preaching as a pastor at Anwoth, and "his pastoral solicitude and his saintly character" as a man devoted to God and His people.

4. Enlarging the Character

Whyte develops his character, Rutherford, by using *examples of his activities, how others viewed him,* and *how he reacted* to situations or other people. Whyte places Rutherford in his typical environment or surroundings, namely his parish at Anwoth. Whyte also describes this unique individual as "a marked man both to the friends and to the enemies of the truth."

---

3. According to William Carson (<http://www.puritansermons.com/ruth/ruth6.htm>):

> Rutherford's preaching was unparalleled. While he was not a good speaker, his preaching drew great attention. ... In 1636 Rutherford published a book defending the doctrines of grace [Calvinism] against Armininism. This put him in conflict with the Church authorities, which were dominated by the English Episcopacy. He was called before the High Court, deprived of his ministerial office, and exiled to Aberdeen. This exile was a sore trial for the beloved pastor. He felt that being separated from his congregation was unbearable. However, because of his exile, we now have many of the letters he wrote to his flock, and so the evil of his banishment has been turned into a great blessing for the church worldwide.
>
> In 1638 the struggles between Parliament and King in England, and Presbyterianism vs. Episcopacy in Scotland culminated in momentous events for Rutherford. In the confusion of the times, he simply slipped out of Aberdeen and returned to his beloved Anwoth. But it was not for long. The Kirk [Church of Scotland] held a General Assembly that year, restoring full Presbyterianism to the land. In addition, they appointed Rutherford a Professor of Theology of St. Andrews, although he negotiated to be allowed to preach at least once a week.
>
> The Westminster Assembly began their famous meetings in 1643, and Rutherford was one of the five Scottish commissioners invited to attend the proceedings. Although the Scots were not allowed to vote, they had an influence far exceeding their number. Rutherford is thought to have been a major influence on the Shorter Catechism. During this period in England, Rutherford wrote his best-known work, "Lex Rex," or "The Law, the King." This book argued for limited government, and limitations on the current idea of the Divine Right of Kings.
>
> When the monarchy was restored in 1660, it was clear that the author of "Lex Rex" could expect trouble. When the summons came in 1661, charging him with treason, and demanding his appearance on a certain day, Rutherford refused to go. From his deathbed, he answered, "I must answer my first summons; and before your day arrives, I will be where few kings and great folks come." He died on 30th March 1661.

Unit 6 Nouns and Pronouns

LESSON 53: NOUNS

✎ EXERCISE A (Page 162)

Spanish forces under Pedro Menéndez de Avilés captured the French Huguenot settlement of Fort Caroline, near present-day Jacksonville, Florida. The French, commanded by René Goulaine de Laudonniere, lost 135 men in the first instance of colonial warfare between European powers in America. Most of those killed were massacred on the order of Avilés, who allegedly had the slain hung on trees beside the inscription: "Not as Frenchmen, but as heretics." Laudonniere and some [forty] other Huguenots escaped. In 1564, the French Huguenots (Protestants) had settled on the Banks of May, a strategic point on the Florida coast. King Philip II of Spain was disturbed by this challenge to Spanish authority in the New World and sent Menéndez de Avilés to Florida to expel the French heretics and establish a Spanish colony there. In early September 1565, Avilés founded San Augustin on the Florida coast, which would later grow into Saint Augustine—the oldest city in North America. Two weeks later, on 20 September, he attacked and destroyed the French settlement of Fort Caroline. The decisive French defeat [compelled] France to refocus its colonial efforts in America far to the north, in what is now Quebec and Nova Scotia in Canada.

✎ EXERCISE B (Page 163)

1. ***Avilés***[a] (appears 4 times)
2. ***Fort Caroline*** (appears twice)
3. ***Jacksonville, Florida***
4. ***French*** (appears twice)
5. ***Laudonniere***[a] (appears twice)
6. ***America*** (appears twice)
7. ***Frenchmen***
8. ***Huguenots***[b] (appears twice)
9. ***Protestants***
10. ***Banks of May***
11. ***King Philip II***
12. ***Spain***
13. ***New World***
14. ***Florida***
15. ***September*** (appears twice)
16. ***San Augustin***
17. ***Saint Augustine***
18. ***North America***
19. ***France***
20. ***Quebec***
21. ***Nova Scotia***
22. ***Canada***

a. Their full names are *Pedro Menéndez de Avilés* and *René Goulaine de Laudonniere*, respectively, and appear in various forms.
b. This proper noun also appears as "French Huguenots."

✎ EXERCISE C (Page 163)

1. ***Pedro Menéndez de Avilés***
2. ***Fort Caroline***
3. ***René Goulaine de Laudonniere***
4. ***warfare***
5. ***Frenchmen***
6. ***French Huguenots***
7. ***Banks of May***
8. ***King Philip II***
9. ***San Augustin***
10. ***Saint Augustine***
11. ***North America***
12. ***Nova Scotia***

✎ EXERCISE D (Page 163)

1. ***forces***
2. ***settlement***
3. ***slain***
4. ***powers***
5. ***colony***
6. ***city***

Teacher: This exercise requires the student to identify only *three* of the above collective nouns.

LESSON 54: PLACING NOUNS

EXERCISE (Page 165)

S — OP — DO
1. The **natives** of **Australia** are called **aborigines.**

PN
2. The natives are **aborigines.**

A — DO
3. Aborigines, **natives** of Australia, use a **weapon** known as a boomerang.

S — IO — DO — OP — OP
4. **Mr. Edwards** told his **grandsons** a **story** about his **experiences** in the **war.**

S — OP — OP — PN
5. The **change** of **caterpillars** into **butterflies** is a fascinating **phenomenon.**

S — PN — OP
6. **Gerald** was chosen **employee** of the **year.**

ADJ. — S — DO — OC
7. The **company president** named **Gerald employee** of the year.

ADJ. — DO
8. Those who are wise experience **wisdom's benefits.**

S — OP — S
9. **Years** passed after the **tragedy,** but the bitter **memories** remained.

ADJ. — S — IO — DO
10. The **music club** offered its **members** more free **selections** than ever before.

LESSON 55: PLURALS OF NOUNS

EXERCISE (Page 169)

1. crutch	*crutches*	11. plaque	*plaques*
2. loaf	*loaves*	12. codex	*codices*
3. bulrush	*bulrushes*	13. capacity	*capacities*
4. Jones	*Joneses*	14. B.S.	*B.S.'s*
5. alto	*altos*	15. notary public	*notary publics*[a]
6. providence	*providences*	16. key	*keys*
7. area	*areas*	17. bureau	*bureaux, bureaus*
8. cockatoo	*cockatoos*	18. Kathy	*Kathys*
9. &, #, +	*&'s, #'s, +'s*	19. grandchild	*grandchildren*
10. plague	*plagues*	20. aide-de-camp	*aides-de-camp*[b]

a. An alternate plural spelling for "notary public" is "notaries public."
b. An alternate plural spelling for "aide-de-camp" is "aids-de-camp."

LESSON 56: MORE ABOUT NOUNS

EXERCISE A (Page 172)

N	1. endorsement	*N*	6. upgrade	*C*	11. writer
N	2. computer	*F*	7. doe (deer)	*M*	12. garçon
F	3. empress	*N*	8. thesaurus	*F*	13. actress
M	4. man	*C*	9. musician	*N*	14. jeans
C	5. referee	*M*	10. master	*N*	15. shoe

✎ EXERCISE B (Page 172)

P 2. They can tolerate another **night's** stay.
O 3. The lines on the **parking lot** need repainting.
N 4. **Earth** is covered mostly with water.
O 5. Give her another **opportunity**.
O 6. Give **Renee** another opportunity.
P 7. Do you have your **parents'** approval?
P 8. He always tries to put in his two **cent's** worth.
O 9. The top of the **building** has an antenna.
N 10. The **top** of the building has an antenna.
O 11. The top of the building has an **antenna**.
N 12. That man is a **relative** of my father.
P 13. The **women's** Bible study meets every Tuesday afternoon.
N 14. My **GameBoy®** needs a new battery.
O 15. My GameBoy® needs a new **battery**.
O 16. She gave the **bellboy** a large tip.

✎ EXERCISE C (Page 173)

branch's[a]	1. branch	*firemen's*	11. firemen
peninsula's	2. peninsula	*Moses'*	12. Moses
father's	3. father	*moth's*	13. moth
lawyers'	4. lawyers	*Sam Cass's*	14. Sam Cass
Mr. Lukes's	5. Mrs. Lukes	*children's*	15. children
doctor's	6. doctor	*confidant's*	16. confidant
Bea and Doris's	7. Bea and Doris	*Aldolphe Sax's*	17. Aldolphe Sax
Australia's	8. Australia	*sectarian's*	18. sectarian
branches'	9. branches	*Edwards'*	19. Edwards
sister-in-law's	10. sister-in-law	*apostles'*	20. apostles

a. The example answer for #1 in the workbook is incorrect; the possessive case for the word *branch* is ***branch's***.

LESSON 57: PRONOUNS

✎ EXERCISE A (Page 175)

1. <u>One</u> never knows <u>what</u> will happen next.
2. <u>Everyone</u> <u>who</u> wants <u>it</u> should simply ask for <u>it</u>.
3. <u>What</u> is the name of the man <u>who</u> spoke to <u>our</u> class?
4. The islands are known for <u>their</u> white beaches, <u>which</u> I hope to visit next year.
5. <u>She</u> cut <u>herself</u> on a sharp blade of grass.
6. <u>He</u> told <u>me</u> <u>what</u> <u>he</u> wanted for <u>his</u> birthday, but <u>I</u> have forgotten <u>what</u> <u>it</u> was.
7. <u>Who</u> is on the Lord's side?
8. To <u>whom</u> was <u>that</u> gift given?

EXERCISE B (Page 176)

Answers will vary.

Teacher: Students are to write a sentence for each of the following types of pronouns: *personal, personal-possessive, compound (reflexive and intensive), interrogative, demonstrative, indefinite,* and *relative.*

LESSON 58: PLACING PRONOUNS

EXERCISE A (Page 179)

N 2. Jay and (he, him) are both going out for basketball.
N 3. Jessica has been ill, but (he, him, she, her) feels better today.
O 4. Mr. Lindstrom told Grant and (I, me) to give our report on euthanasia.
N 5. (We, Us) girls are planning a slumber party.
N 6. "Hello! Is Brian home?" … "Yes, this is (he, him)."
N 7. The ROTC commander is (he, him).
P 8. Everyone should pay (his, her, their) own way.
N 9. (They, Them) and (we, us) are facing off in the tournament.
N 10. The sparring partners were Manuel and (she, her).
P 11. Both men were cognizant of (his, their) roles in the offense.
N 12. May Joni and (I, me) order a pizza tonight?
N 13. Do you and (him, he) expect to graduate?
O 14. Give (she, her) a portion of the business.
N 15. God (Himself, Hisself) will be with you forever.

EXERCISE B (Page 180)

CASE ➡	Nominative		Objective	
NUMBER ➡	Singular	Plural	Singular	Plural
First Person	*I*	*we*	*me*	*us*
Second Person	*you*	*you*	*you*	*you*
Third Person	*he, she, it*	*they*	*him, her, it*	*them*

LESSON 59: UNIT REVIEW

EXERCISE A (Page 180)

1. ***Proper*** nouns are always capitalized.
2. A ***pronoun*** is a word that is used as a noun substitute.
3. Name the seven types of *pronouns*:

a. ***Personal***
b. ***Personal-possessive***
c. ***Compound***
d. ***Interrogative***
e. ***Demonstrative***
f. ***Indefinite***
g. ***Relative***

4. *Answers will vary.*

Teacher: The student is required to write a 75-word paragraph using various kinds of *nouns* and *pronouns.*

---

5. *Answers will vary.*

Teacher: For problem #5, the student is required to list an example of each of the four kinds of *nouns* and eight kinds of *pronouns* found in the paragraph written for #4 above.

✎ EXERCISE B (Page 181)

1. What is a substantive?

   A substantive is a term that may be used to refer to any word, phrase, or clause that has the qualities and uses of a noun. In its capacity as a noun (to name persons, places, things, qualities, or ideas), a substantive can be used in the seven following ways: subject, direct object, indirect object, object of preposition, objective complement, predicate nominative, and appositive.
2. A ***subject*** is a substantive about which a sentence makes a statement.
3. An ***objective complement*** is a substantive (or adjective) used after a direct object to complete its meaning.
4. ***Number*** is the grammatical term indicating whether a part of speech refers to one or more than one.
5. The plural of nouns ending with a *-y* preceded by a consonant is formed by ***changing the "y" to "i" and adding -es.***
6. How many genders are possible for English nouns? ***4*** They are: ***masculine, feminine, neuter, and common.***
7. The three cases of English nouns are: ***nominative***, ***objective***, and ***possessive***.
8. Nouns used as *subjects* and *predicate nominatives* are in the ***nominative*** case.

   Nouns used as *objects* are in the ***objective*** case.

   Nouns that show *ownership* are in the ***possessive*** case.
9. The indefinite pronouns that are always plural are ***both***, ***few***, ***several***, and ***many***.

Unit 7 Verbs, Verbals, and Participles

LESSON 60: VERBS

✎ EXERCISE A (Page 185)

2. It has (*H*) been (*H*) said (*A*) that he who does (*H*) not plan (*A*) for the future will (*H*) be (*S*) woebegone—beset (*A*) by woes.
3. Today you broke (*A*) my heart in a place that was (*H*) not broken (*A*).
4. Actions speak (*A*) louder than words.
5. "For by one Spirit we were (*H*) all baptized (*A*) into one body" (1 Corinthians 12:13a).
6. The theory of evolution is (*L*) one of the greatest evidences of man's rebellion against God.

A L
7. Someone once wrote that the two greatest "abilities" are availability and dependability.

A
8. The team commemorated its outstanding season by honoring its coach.

H A
9. Each year they have given us a bonus at the end of the year.

H H A S H A
10. It could be said that things are not always as we would have them.

✎ EXERCISE B (Page 186)

T
2. Sue assembled all the parts for her science project.

T
3. A DVD will generate a clearer picture than a video will.

I I (does run)
4. Either he runs to win or he does not run at all.

I I (does repay) T I
5. "The wicked borrows and does not repay, but the righteous shows mercy and gives" (Psalms 37:21).

T
6. God shines the light of His Gospel over the whole earth.

I
7. Steve only flew over well-charted routes.

I
8. My father works for a not-for-profit ministry.

T
9. The student delivered his speech in front of the entire school body.

I T
10. "For the earth shall be full of the knowledge of the LORD as the waters cover the sea" (Isaiah 11:9).

LESSON 61: PLACING VERBS

✎ EXERCISE A (Page 191)

2. Please, do not hesitate to call.

Tense: 1	*Voice:* 1	*Tone:* 3	*Mood:* 2

3. The eucalyptus leaves were eaten by a koala bear.

Tense: 2	*Voice:* 2	*Tone:* 1	*Mood:* 1

4. Please do not shout at each other.

Tense: 1	*Voice:* 1	*Tone:* 3	*Mood:* 2

5. Dave has been laying tile in our home.

Tense: 4	*Voice:* 1	*Tone:* 2	*Mood:* 1

6. She will have been waiting for an hour.

Tense: 6	*Voice:* 1	*Tone:* 2	*Mood:* 1

7. The play had been seen by several hundred students.

Tense: 5	*Voice:* 2	*Tone:* 1	*Mood:* 1

8. We shall not be affected by mere emotion.

Tense: 3	Voice: 2	Tone: 1	Mood: 1

9. They were being deceived by the liberal media.

Tense: 2	Voice: 2	Tone: 2	Mood: 1

10. Thy will be done, Lord.

Tense: 1	Voice: 2	Tone: 1	Mood: 3

✎ **EXERCISE B (Page 192)**

2. *God's Word was faithfully taught to the youth by Jerry.*
3. *Her peers are awarding her.*
4. *The Web page was produced by Bob in a few hours.*
5. *At all times, the elders are shepherding the congregants.*
6. *The hymn "O Father, You Are Sovereign" was written by E. Margaret Clarkson.*
7. *The drama club achieved a memorable performance during the fall semester.*
8. *The congregation will provide some of her expenses as a missionary.*

LESSON 62: VERBALS

✎ **EXERCISE A (Page 194)**

	INFINITIVE	GERUND	PRESENT PARTICIPLE	PAST PARTICIPLE
2. display	*to display*	*displaying*	*displaying*	*displayed*
3. spoil	*to spoil*	*spoiling*	*spoiling*	*spoiled*
4. anger	*to anger*	*angering*	*angering*	*angered*
5. dispute	*to dispute*	*disputing*	*disputing*	*disputed*
6. fancy	*to fancy*	*fancying*	*fancying*	*fancied*
7. continue	*to continue*	*continuing*	*continuing*	*continued*
8. guess	*to guess*	*guessing*	*guessing*	*guessed*
9. bewilder	*to bewilder*	*bewildering*	*bewildering*	*bewildered*
10. scurry	*to scurry*	*scurrying*	*scurrying*	*scurried*

✎ **EXERCISE B (Page 195)**

Hint: To decide whether an *-ing* word is a present participle or a gerund, you will have to decide whether it is used as a noun (*gerund*) or adjective (*present participle*).

G 2. **Glorifying** God is man's chief end.

PP 3. My family ate **barbecued** burgers around the picnic table.

PS 4. The chicken casserole was served in a **baking** dish.

G 5. **Buying** time was his only hope of escape.

I 6. She needed **to collect** (*N*) her thoughts.

I 7. The geologists searched for fossils **to collect**. (*ADJ.*)

I 8. Jessica was ready **to execute** her plan. (*ADV.*)

PP 9. He received his information from a **posted** news bulletin.

PS 10. The Gregorian order is renowned for its **chanting** monks.

EXERCISE C (Page 195)

Answers will vary.

LESSON 63: PRINCIPAL PARTS OF VERBS

EXERCISE A (Page 200)

Note: The student should memorize the principal parts of the *irregular verbs* in the table in the ***Appendix***.

EXERCISE B (Page 200)

First	Second	Third	Fourth
2. spin	*spinning*	*spun*	*spun*
3. see	*seeing*	*saw*	*seen*
4. give	*giving*	*gave*	*given*
5. worry	*worrying*	*worried*	*worried*
6. spy	*spying*	*spied*	*spied*
7. mean	*meaning*	*meant*	*meant*
8. burn	*burning*	*burned, burnt*	*burned, burnt*
9. taint	*tainting*	*tainted*	*tainted*
10. shake	*shaking*	*shook*	*shaken*
11. lie (recline)	*lying*	*lay*	*lain*
12. cover	*covering*	*covered*	*covered*
13. fumble	*fumbling*	*fumbled*	*fumbled*
14. worship	*worship(p)ing*	*worship(p)ed*	*worship(p)ed*

EXERCISE C (Page 201)

Teacher: *Answers will vary*, but sample answers are given below to show the correct verb form.

1. **show**: *past tense, passive voice, simple tone*
   The students ***were shown*** *the inner working of a computer.*
2. **speak**: *present perfect tense, active voice, progressive tone*
   They ***have been speaking*** *about the design for an hour.*
3. **choose**: *past perfect tense, passive voice, simple tone*
   The mayor ***had been chosen*** *by a special municipal election.*
4. **eat**: *past tense, active voice, emphatic tone*
   The guys ***did eat*** *a lot at the sports banquet.*

5. **bite**: *present perfect tense, passive voice, simple tone*
   He ***has been bitten*** *by several yellow jackets, which may be fatal.*
6. **steal**: *present tense, active voice, emphatic tone, imperative mood*
   Do *not* ***steal*** *words or ideas from someone else; that is plagiarism.*

LESSON 64: UNIT REVIEW

✎ EXERCISE A (Page 201)

1. The four main *types of verbs* are:
   a. ***Action verbs*** c. ***State-of-being verbs***
   b. ***Helping verbs*** d. ***Linking verbs***
2. ***Tense*** is a grammatical term signifying the time frame in which the action or condition expressed by a verb takes place.
3. Write the *six tenses* of the verb "to be," using the first person singular form:
   I am (Present) ***I have been (Present Perfect)***
   I was (Past) ***I had been (Past Perfect)***
   I shall be (Future) ***I shall have been (Future Perfect)***
4. The *three tones* of English verbs are ***simple***, ***progressive***, and ***emphatic***.
5. When the subject is the doer of the action, the verb is in ***active*** voice. When the subject is the receiver of the action, the verb is in ***passive*** voice.
6. *Mood* is the grammatical term indicating the ***state of mind*** or ***manner*** in which a statement is being made by a verb. The *three moods* of English verbs are ***indicative, imperative, and subjunctive***.
7. Verbs used as another part of speech are called ***verbals***.The three types are ***participles (present and past), infinitives, and gerunds.***
8. *Infinitives* may be used as ***nouns, adjectives, or adverbs***.
9. *Gerunds* are used as ***nouns***.
10. *Participles* are used as ***adjectives***.
11. The *four principal parts* of verbs are ***present***, ***present participle***, ***past***, and ***past participle***.
12. *Answers will vary.*

Teacher: The student is required to write a paragraph of about 75 words using at least three of each of the following: *verbs*, *verbals*, and *participial phrases*.

---

13. *Answers will vary.*

Teacher: For problem #13, the student is required to list three *verbs*, two *verbals*, and three *participles* (or *participial phrases*, which is the intent of the exercise) found in the paragraph written for #12 above.

✎ EXERCISE B (Page 203)

1. The thief stole (*I*) from the convenience store but, in haste, left (*T*) incriminating evidence behind.
2. The church choir will perform (*T*) the cantata before the congregation.

3. His poem was read (T) by his literature teacher.

4. So you care (T) deeply for the lost, or you do (I) not care at all.

5. The satellite beamed (T) information gathered by the astronauts in the space station.

6. She walked (I) to Starbucks for a cup of coffee, where she ran into (T) a friend from work.

7. The missionary challenged (T) the young people to "put feet to their faith."

✎ EXERCISE C (Page 203)

Number ➠	Singular	Plural
Tense ➠	***Present***	
First Person	**I** *begin*	**we** *begin*
Second Person	**you** *begin*	**you** *begin*
Third Person	**he (she, it)** *begins*	**they** *begin*
Tense ➠	***Past***	
First Person	**I** *began*	**we** *began*
Second Person	**you** *began*	**you** *began*
Third Person	**he (she, it)** *began*	**they** *began*
Tense ➠	***Future***	
First Person	**I** *shall begin*	**we** *shall begin*
Second Person	**you** *will begin*	**you** *will begin*
Third Person	**he (she, it)** *will begin*	**they** *will begin*
Tense ➠	***Present Perfect***	
First Person	**I** *have begun*	**we** *have begun*
Second Person	**you** *have begun*	**you** *have begun*
Third Person	**he (she, it)** *has begun*	**they** *have begun*
Tense ➠	***Past Perfect***	
First Person	**I** *had begun*	**we** *had begun*
Second Person	**you** *had begun*	**you** *had begun*
Third Person	**he (she, it)** *had begun*	**they** *had begun*
Tense ➠	***Future Perfect***	
First Person	**I** *shall have begun*	**we** *shall have begun*
Second Person	**you** *will have begun*	**you** *will have begun*
Third Person	**he (she, it)** *will have begun*	**they** *will have begun*

✎ EXERCISE D (Page 204)

MOOD ➠	INDICATIVE		SUBJUNCTIVE	
Number ➠	**Singular**	**Plural**	**Singular**	**Plural**
***Tense* ➠**	***Present***			
First Person	I *am*	we *are*	(if) I *be*	(if) we *be*
Second Person	you *are*	you *are*	(if) you *be*	(if) you *be*
Third Person	he (she, it) *is*	they *are*	(if) he (she, it) *be*	(if) they *be*
***Tense* ➠**	***Past***			
First Person	I *was*	we *were*	(if) I *were*	(if) we *were*
Second Person	you *were*	you *were*	(if) you *were*	(if) you *were*
Third Person	he (she, it) *was*	they *were*	(if) he (she, it) *were*	(if) they *were*
***Tense* ➠**	***Future***			
First Person	I *shall be*	we *shall be*	(if) I *shall be*	(if) we *shall be*
Second Person	you *will be*	you *will be*	(if) you *will be*	(if) you *will be*
Third Person	he (she, it) *will be*	they *will be*	(if) he (she, it) *will be*	(if) they *will be*

✎ EXERCISE E (Page 204)

First	Second	Third	Fourth
1. wake	*waking*	*waked, woke*	*(have) waked, woken*
2. read	*reading*	*read*	*(have) read*
3. blink	*blinking*	*blinked*	*(have) blinked*
4. take	*taking*	*took*	*(have) taken*
5. envy	*envying*	*envied*	*(have) envied*
6. bid (command)	*bidding*	*bade, bid*	*(have) bidden, bid*
7. drink	*drinking*	*drank*	*(have) drunk, drunken*

Unit 8 Five Other Parts of Speech

LESSON 65: ADJECTIVES

✎ EXERCISE A (Page 206)

2. The football team scored several goals during the second half of the game.

3. The ambitious woman seemed fond of using remarks to portray rivals' ideas as nocuous.

4. A simple adjective is usually placed immediately before the word it modifies.

5. Eric was convinced that the theological argument would persuade the most incredulous skeptic.

6. Wars, foreign and domestic, have taken the lives of many young American men.

✎ **EXERCISE B (Page 207)**

	ADJECTIVE UNDERLINED	WORD MODIFIED	TYPE OF ADJECTIVE
2.	*football*	*team*	*SA*
	several	*goals*	*SA*
	second	*half*	*SA*
3.	*ambitious*	*woman*	*SA*
	fond	*woman*	*PA*
	rivals'	*ideas*	*SA*
	nocuous	*ideas*	*OC*
4.	*simple*	*adjective*	*SA*
5.	*theological*	*argument*	*SA*
	incredulous	*skeptic*	*SA*
6.	*foreign*	*Wars*	*AA*
	domestic	*Wars*	*AA*
	many	*men*	*SA*
	young	*men*	*SA*
	American	*men*	*PRO. ADJ.*

LESSON 66: ADVERBS

✎ **EXERCISE (Page 208)**

1. That was the most precious gift she had ever received.
2. The moon appeared suddenly in the sky as they spryly hiked through the mountains.
3. The prospectus almost always outlines the company's projected earnings.
4. Jesus was always sympathetic toward the needy.
5. Anxiously the wives of the trapped miners awaited news of their rescue.
6. The boys eagerly looked forward to learning the manly art of self-defense.
7. The negotiators said they were cautiously optimistic about the outcome of their talks.

LESSON 67: PREPOSITIONS

✎ **EXERCISE (Page 210)**

1. He makes me to lie down in green pastures.
2. He leads me beside the still waters.
3. He leads me in the paths of righteousness for His name's sake.
4. Yea, though I walk through the valley of the shadow of death, I will fear no evil; for You are with me.
5. You prepare a table before me in the presence of my enemies.

6. You anoint my head with oil.
7. Surely goodness and mercy shall follow me all the days of my life.
8. I shall dwell in the house of the Lord forever.
9. The preceding sentences were all taken from Psalm 23.

LESSON 68: CONJUNCTIONS

✎ EXERCISE (Page 212)

CA
C 2. Your term paper is excellent; furthermore, you could submit it for publication.

Sub.
C 3. Some people act as if they own the world.

Sub.
C 4. As long as you are donating the car, why don't you donate it to me?

Sub.
C 5. Although he was young, Timothy was an effective witness for the Gospel.

CC *CC*
C 6. Either you are with me or you are against me.

CC *CC*
W 7. Both Rita and Mary Anne flew to Montreal for the conference.

SC
W 8. George W. Bush and Richard B. Cheney were running mates in 2000.

SC
C 9. June was a "civil" person, but her actions betrayed her true personality.

Sub.
C 10. You cannot go until you finish your homework assignment.

Teacher: Note that the term "neither" may be used as a *simple conjunction* rather than a *correlative*. As a simple conjunction, *neither* is used in the same sense as *nor* when it follows some other negative such as *no, not,* or *never*. By definition, *neither* is considered a correlative conjunction only if it is used in pairs (e.g., *neither … nor*).

LESSON 69: INTERJECTIONS, ETC.

✎ EXERCISE (Page 213)

Answers will vary.

Teacher: The student is to write four sentences using *interjections* and four sentences using *nouns of direct address*.

LESSON 70: UNIT REVIEW

✎ EXERCISE A (Page 214)

1. ***Adjectives*** modify nouns or pronouns; ***adverbs*** modify verbs, adjectives, or other ***adverbs***.
2. A group of words beginning with a preposition and ending with a noun or pronoun is called a ***prepositional phrase***.

3. What are the two main classifications of *conjunctions*?

   a. ***Coordinating*** b. ***Subordinating***

4. What three types of words can be used to connect sentence elements that are of equal grammatical rank?

   a. ***Simple conjunctions*** b. ***Correlative conjunctions*** c. ***Conjunctive adverbs***

5. Give four examples of *interjections*. (*Answers will vary. See chart on page 213 in the workbook.*)

   a. ***Ouch!*** b. ***Phooey!*** c. ***Oh, my!*** d. ***Behold!***

6. *Answers will vary.*

Teacher: The student is required to write a paragraph of 75 words or less using each of the *eight parts of speech.*

---

7. *Answers will vary.*

Teacher: For problem #7, the student is required to list three examples of each of the *eight parts of speech* found in the paragraph written for #6 above.

EXERCISE B (Page 215)

P V N
2. **His** report needs to be **submitted** by the **end** of the week.

P Adv. Adj.
3. **Your** account will be activated **automatically** by pressing **the** return key.

P Adv. Prep.
4. **She** does **not** want to come **for** the holiday.

N C V Prep.
5. Obeying the **Bible** may be difficult, **but** it **will lead** you in the way of salvation **in** the end.

Int. N N Prep. P
6. **Wow!** What **kind** of attitude the **children** have displayed **before us**!

P Adv. Adj.
7. **I** am **only** trying to be **practical**.

Adv. Adj. Prep. C Adv.
8. They were **entirely mistaken concerning** what he did; **however**, they were **likely** misinformed.

Adj. N Prep. Adj.
9. The **agile**, brown **antelope** jumped away **from** the **crouching** lion's hideout.

P Adv. N
10. **Those** species of creatures **usually** exhibit an incredible **means** of survival.

P Adj. V N
11. **It** is **easy** to see where she **got** her good **looks**.

P V Adj. Prep.
12. **My** cousin **works** for a **large** media company **in** the Loop.

N Adv. Prep.
13. The **train** will be stopping **automatically** at each station **during** rush hour.

Adj. P Prep.
14. She was a **thoughtful** person **who** was well-liked **by** her colleagues.

N Adj. C N
15. "Sweatin' to the **Oldies**" may be **amusing, but** it makes **exercising** fun.

V Adj. Adv. Adv.
16. **Tell** me! Why did your **Op-Ed** piece **not** appear in the paper **today**?

V N P Adj.
17. Ted **ordered** his staff to roll the **press**, but **they** were not **ready** to start.

Adv. Prep. P C V Adv.
18. He was **totally** embarrassed **about** what **they** said; **yet**, they kept **badgering** him **unmercifully**.

Adj. N Adv. N V
19. The **tall**, heavy **man** waddled **over** to the **chair** to **rest** his legs.

P V N Prep. N
20. **What** set of books **does** the **child** want **for** his **birthday**?

Teacher: For grading purposes, there are 75 items that need to be identified in this exercise.

Unit 9 Phrases and Clauses

LESSON 71: PHRASES

✎ EXERCISE A (Page 219)

2. **Practicing daily** is the smart way to increase your music skills. ***Ger.***
3. Henry tried **to convince him immediately**. ***Inf.***
4. The girl **combing her hair** is my sister. ***Part.***
5. **Putting feet to your faith** is the best way to fulfill the Great Commission. ***Ger.***
6. **Do** you always **tell** the truth? ***V.***
7. We ordered ten copies **of the book** from the publisher. ***Prep.***
8. *Hamlet* **has been seen** by countless people. ***V.***
9. The time **to bow the knee** to God is now. ***Inf.***
10. **From the airport** we will go home. ***Prep.***
11. Washington crossed the river **to attack the British**. ***Inf.***
12. One difficulty of **becoming a missionary** is learning a new language. ***Ger.***
13. One difficulty of becoming a missionary is **learning a new language**. ***Ger.***
14. One difficulty **of becoming a missionary** is learning a new language. ***Prep.***
15. The man **learning a new language** is a missionary. ***Part.***

✎ EXERCISE B (Page 220)

A
3. ___*N*___ His dream, **to become a surgeon**, will require many years of schooling.

4. ___*V*___ He **will be coming** on the weekend.

S
5. ___*N*___ **To be a successful entrepreneur** takes more perspiration than inspiration.

6. ___*Adv.*___ **To be a successful entrepreneur**, he knew he needed to work hard.

7. *Adj.* **Being a successful entrepreneur,** he devoted himself to his business.

8. *N* **Being a successful entrepreneur** (*S*) gave him the ability to support many missionaries.

9. *N* By **winning second place** (*OP*), the Olympian received a silver medal.

10. *Adv.* His philosophy is difficult **to explain simply**.

11. *Adv.* He does not make enough **to save for retirement**.

12. *N* Benjamin learned the art of **folding paper** (*OP*), known as origami.

13. *N* I must stop **eating late at night** (*DO*).

14. *Adv.* Are you smart enough **to pass this exam**?

15. *N* **Going to church** (*S*) does not make you a Christian any more than being baptized does.

LESSON 72: CLAUSES

✎ EXERCISE A (Page 224)

N 2. Ask me which commandment is the first with a promise.
Adj. 3. Aaron is the one who is wearing a white shirt and tie.
N 4. That she is dedicated to our cause is quite clear from her actions.
Adv. 5. I am dismayed that you thought it necessary to remind me of my duty.
Adv. 6. While I was waiting, I did my homework.
N 7. She would not reveal which person was responsible for the debacle.
Adj. 8. As bright as he was, Professor Nash had few social skills.
Adv. 9. When he awoke, he could not remember much.
N 10. When he awoke could not be ascertained.

✎ EXERCISE B (Page 224)

DO 2. Please tell me what you think.
DO 3. I often cannot tell what you think.
OP 4. She told me about what you think.
PN 5. So this is what you think!
A 6. An important fact—what you think—has been ignored by all of them.
S 7. How you care has been ignored by all of them.

✎ EXERCISE C (Page 224)

DO 2. Serving is what the soldier enjoyed the most.
Adj. 3. This brave man, whose vehicle was strafed, was not wounded in the crossfire.

Adv. 4. He dared not tell us how he arranged to elude the enemy.

X 5. He convinced us that all would be fine.

S 6. He did whatever was necessary to escape.

Adv. 7. That is why he was chosen to lead our outfit.

✎ **EXERCISE D (Page 225)**

2. A Christian is a person (whose sins have been forgiven by God through Christ).
3. A Christian is a person (for whom Christ died).
4. (Whether you have faith in Christ) is essential to your salvation.
5. (Unless you are eighteen years old), you cannot vote in the upcoming election.
6. We visited the battlefield (where Custer and his men died).
7. "(If you love Me), keep My commandments."
8. Jesus is the Savior (whose blood covers all the sins) ({that} I have ever committed).

LESSON 73: UNIT REVIEW

✎ **EXERCISE A (Page 225)**

1. A phrase is ***a group of related words, containing neither a subject nor a predicate. A phrase does not express a complete thought in itself.***
2. Phrases may be classified according to ***their function*** or according to ***their structure***.
3. As to function, phrases may be used as ***nouns***, ***verbs***, ***adjectives***, or ***adverbs***.
4. The five main categories of phrases, as to structure, are ***prepositional***, ***verb***, ***participial***, ***gerundial***, and ***infinitive***.
5. A prepositional phrase consists of ***a group of words beginning with a preposition and ending with a substantive called the object of the preposition.***
6. A verb phrase consists of ***a main verb and all of its helping verbs***.
7. A participial phrase consists of ***a participle and any related complements and modifiers***.
8. A gerundial phrase consists of ***a gerund and any related complements and modifiers***.
9. An infinitive phrase consists of ***an infinitive and any related complements and modifiers***.
10. A clause is ***a group of words containing both a subject and a verb and used as a part of a sentence***.
11. The three types of dependent clauses are ***noun***, ***adjective***, and ***adverb***.
12. Adverb clauses are introduced by ***subordinating conjunctions***.
13. Noun clauses are introduced by ***signal words***.
14. Adjective clauses are introduced by ***relatives***.
15. In regard to adjective clauses, the introductory words *who*, *whom*, *which*, and *that* are examples of relative ***pronouns***; *whose* and *which* are examples of relative ***adjectives***; *and when* and *where* are examples of relative ***adverbs***.

✎ **EXERCISE B (Page 226)**

1. *N* My goal, **to complete** *A* **the manuscript**, will take several months.
2. *Adj.* **Being an ardent fan**, he followed the team tenaciously.

3. *Adj.* The ship **sailing the high seas** was heading for safe harbor.

4. *N* By **choosing the path of least resistance**, the sluggard missed many opportunities. (*OP*)

5. *N* **To be a godly example** requires much prayer and meekness. (*S*)

6. *Adv.* Their ideology is hard **to define in absolute terms**.

7. *N* Professor Carson enjoys **reading theological tomes**. (*DO*)

8. *N* **Being a merciful person** gave her the capacity to love the unlovable. (*S*)

9. *V* The secretary of state **will be meeting** with the Saudis over the next few days.

10. *Adj.* **To be an effective leader**, he knew he had to earn the people's trust.

✎ **EXERCISE C (Page 226)**

S 1. Whom the pastor married was the most godly couple in the church.
OP 2. Peter told me about what you did.
Adv. 3. Although he was reluctant, he still sang in the chorus.
PN 4. My question is whether you are ready to meet the challenge.
A 5. The most direct route, where we take I-294, was the most crowded.
Adv. 6. You must play smart, if you are going to win the game.
Adj. 7. She will be the one who is carrying the briefcase and wearing a scarf.
S 8. That we are always in the dark is obvious.
Adj. 9. The report that you filed was the wrong one.
DO 10. He could not discern which person was telling the truth.

Unit 10 Sentences

LESSON 74: COMMON SENTENCE ERRORS

✎ **EXERCISE (Page 229)** *Completion of sentence fragments will vary.*

R 2. *Trust in the LORD with all your heart, and lean not on your own understanding.* (NKJV)
OR *Trust in the LORD with all [thine] heart; and lean not [unto thine] own understanding.* (KJV)
F 3. *The elder who oversees missions will introduce a new missionary candidate.*
R 4. *Remember our trip to Australia? What a wonderful time we had!*
F 5. *Using all those suggestions is impossible at this time.*
F 6. *The transplant surgery that Dr. Koffron performed was successful.*
F 7. *Whatever you were about to do, you should begin by organizing your time.*
R 8. *Perhaps you should take that course since it meets one of your graduation requirements.*
OR *Perhaps you should take that course; it meets one of your graduation requirements.*

R 9. *Jesus wept. Then the Jews said, "See how He loved him!"* (NKJV)
F 10. *I gazed at the bald eagle majestically soaring through the sky.*
OR *The bald eagle majestically soaring through the sky was awe-inspiring.*

LESSON 75: CORRECTING FAULTY COORDINATION

EXERCISE A (Page 231)

choice 1. Shape up ***or*** ship out!
addition 2. Jed planned the expedition***, and*** Art was his right-hand man.
result 3. In 1893, economic depression caused widespread unrest***; therefore,*** (or ***; consequently,***) this prompted calls for a more pervasive government role in managing the economy—the seedling of our modern welfare state.
choice 4. Call a meeting of the board immediately***, or*** (or ***; otherwise,***) I will resign my position.
addition 5. The fear of the Lord is the beginning of wisdom***, and*** the knowledge of the Holy One is understanding. (NKJV)
contrast 6. The Red Cross brought disaster relief to many victims of catastrophes***, but*** (or ***; however,***) they still received numerous requests for help.
result 7. God has justified believers by faith***; therefore,*** (or ***; consequently,***) they have peace with Him through Christ.
contrast 8. The professor gave the class detailed instructions***, but*** (or ***; however,***) the students did not understand.

EXERCISE B (Page 233)

condition 1. You will not be saved, ***unless*** you repent of your sins and believe in Christ.
purpose 2. Please clear your things off the table ***in order that*** (or ***so that***) I can set it for supper.
time 3. ***When*** (or ***After***) everyone had arrived, we started the Bible study.
cause 4. We had to return home quickly ***since*** (or ***because***) we forgot to lock the door.

EXERCISE C (Page 233) *Answers will vary. Sample answers are given in bold print.*

2. ***Unless I finish all my homework,*** *I will not be able to go on the winter retreat.*
OR *I will not be able to go on the winter retreat* ***because I need to stay with my dad while he is ill.***
3. *Mark began to organize a work day at church* ***when he saw how much work needed to be done.***
OR ***When the trustees decided to paint the sanctuary,*** *Mark began to organize a work day at church.*
4. ***When one of the clan returned from Santiago, Chile,*** *the Cassidys decided to have a family reunion.*
OR *The Cassidys decided to have a family reunion* ***after Papa Cassidy turned 100 years old.***
5. *The pastor encouraged his congregation to vote in the next election* ***since it was their duty.***
OR ***When November arrived,*** *the pastor encouraged his congregation to vote in the next election.*
6. ***If the courts charge them with "racketeering,"*** *pro-life activists may be barred from protesting.*
OR *Pro-life activists may be barred from protesting* ***if abortionists get their way.***
7. *Missionaries need to learn the local dialect* ***if they are going to reach people with the Gospel.***
OR ***Since the mission board requires language proficiency,*** *missionaries need to learn the local dialect.*

✎ **EXERCISE D (Page 234)**

1. *Elector Frederick III,* **who was one of the most powerful German princes,** *governed the Palatinate.*
2. *Zacharius Ursinus and Caspar Olevianus,* **who were two theological professors at Heidelberg University,** *formulated the Heidelberg Catechism.*
3. *The catechism,* **which was approved by a synod in Heidelberg in January 1563,** *was later divided into fifty-two sections for exposition during Sunday services throughout the year.*
4. *The Heidelberg Catechism,* **which soon became the most ecumenical of the Reformed catechisms,** *was also approved by the Synod of Dort in 1618–1619.*
5. *The catechism,* **which is the most widely used and most warmly praised catechism of the Reformation period,** *is the most translated of all Reformation catechisms.*

✎ **EXERCISE E (Page 236)** ***Answers may vary. Sample answers are given in bold print.***

Place the subordinate idea in a subordinate adjective or adverb clause:

1. *Iraq,* **which is located along the Tigris and Euphrates rivers,** *was once under British administration.*

OR *Iraq,* **which was once under British administration,** *is located along the Tigris and Euphrates rivers.*

2. ***Though*** *Mr. Morello taught high school art for a number of years, he now owns his own gallery.*

OR *Mr. Morello,* **who taught high school art for a number of years,** *now owns his own gallery.*

3. ***After*** *she waited at the dentist's office for an hour, the doctor finally called her.*

Place the subordinate idea in a modifying phrase:

4. *The call* **to surrender** *came from General Lee.*
5. *The congregation* **accommodating the rich and powerful** *teetered on the edge of demise.*
6. *Steve was looking for an employee* **who must be willing to work fast and furiously.**

Place the subordinate idea in an appositive:

7. *Joshua is joining the pro-life alliance,* ***an extremely vital association.***
8. *Grisham's latest novel,* **The King of Torts,** *is written in the same propelling style that has made his legal thrillers so accessible.*
9. *Mrs. Castle,* ***our grandmother,*** *emigrated from Luxembourg over twenty years ago.*

LESSON 76: PRONOUN AND ANTECEDENT AGREEMENT

✎ **EXERCISE (Page 238)** ***Answers will vary. Sample answers are given in bold print.***

Revise by correcting ambiguous references:

1. *I overheard Gavin talking to Ethan about* ***Ethan's*** *new Diggler's Dirt-Dawg.*

OR *I overheard Gavin talking to Ethan about* ***Gavin's*** *new Diggler's Dirt-Dawg.*

2. *The dry cleaner pressed my suits after she removed the stains.*
3. *Although Rita had met the new doctor previously,* ***the doctor*** *did not remember her.*

OR *Although Rita had met the new doctor previously,* ***Rita*** *did not remember her.*

Revise by correcting general references:

4. *Since Dad never gets around to fixing the dryer, Mom cannot do the laundry; and she is tired of* ***this problem.***
5. *The girls fight like cats and dogs,* ***a proclivity*** *which their father abhors.*

6. *Missionaries showed a film of their work, spoke of the desperate plight of the believers in Sudan, and challenged us to help.* ***His presentation*** *moved the congregation.*

Revise by correcting weak references:

7. *After teaching a year at the mission school, Esther decided she didn't want to be* ***a teacher.***
8. *The Great Barrier Reef was well worth seeing, but* ***a tour*** *would take several days.*

OR *The Great Barrier Reef was well worth seeing, but it would take several days* ***to see it.***

9. *Intoxicated by the rocky Mediterranean landscape, Cézanne painted prolifically; but he was increasingly unable to detach himself from* ***his paintings,*** *owing to his passionate temperament.*

Revise by correcting the indefinite use of *it, they,* and *you*:

10. *According to an article in the* Guardian Unlimited, ***the author*** *claimed that, after the UN weapons inspectors left in 1998, the sole source of intelligence concerning Saddam's regime was the Iraqi National Congress—a London-based, dissident group.*
11. *During the Dark Ages,* ***the people*** *lived under miserable conditions.*
12. *In polite conversation* ***a person doesn't*** *talk about the problems* ***he faces*** *at home.*

LESSON 77: PLACEMENT OF MODIFIERS

EXERCISE A (Page 240) ***Answers will vary. Sample answers are given in bold print.***

1. *On Wednesday evening, the church offers an Awana program* ***starting at 6:30*** *for children.*
2. *One of my buddies went to Aspen* ***so he could go rock climbing with his new gear.***

OR ***With his new gear,*** *one of my buddies went to Aspen so he could go rock climbing.*

3. *The students began to have major conflicts* ***with their teacher*** *about the scores they had received.*
4. ***After we confronted him,*** *Brett finally admitted "borrowing" Anne's car.*

OR *Brett finally admitted,* ***after we confronted him,*** *that he "borrowed" Anne's car.*

5. *The animated classic is about a poor little girl* ***named Penny*** *who lives in an orphanage.*

OR *The animated classic* ***named Penny*** *is about a poor little girl who lived in an orphanage.*

6. ***Since he underestimated his opponent,*** *the lawyer digressed from the argument he had developed.*

OR *The lawyer,* ***having underestimated his opponent,*** *digressed from the argument he had developed.*

7. *At Tuesday's meeting, the treasurer discussed* ***with the association members*** *the considerable cost of repairing the townhouse roofs.*

OR *At Thursday's meeting* ***with the association members,*** *the treasurer discussed the considerable cost of repairing the townhouse roofs.*

8. *Jan followed* ***with concern*** *the controversy over the expansion of O'Hare International Airport.*

OR ***With concern,*** *Jan followed the controversy over the expansion of O'Hare International Airport.*

EXERCISE B (Page 242) ***Answers will vary. Sample answers are given in bold print.***

1. ***When someone is*** *learning a new software program, the menus must be explored.*
2. *After listening to the Pharisees' remarks,* ***Jesus*** *gave an astonishing reply.*
3. *Standing near the mechanic,* ***the man*** *was struck by a metal burr.*
4. ***As we were driving to church,*** *the traffic lights were all green.*
5. *Having promised to be home by 10:00,* ***I*** *caused my father concern when I arrived at midnight.*
6. *Clear*
7. *Embarrassed by her childish attitude,* ***she*** *changed her opinion by week's end.*

✎ **EXERCISE C (Page 243)**

1. ***Before the vote was taken,*** *Mr. Bennett wanted to know what the officials said to his opponent.*

OR *Mr. Bennett wanted to know what the officials said to his opponent* ***before the vote was taken.***

2. ***When he finishes the lawn,*** *tell Scott I want to talk to him.*

OR *Tell Scott I want to talk to him* ***when he finishes the lawn.***

3. ***After the sixth inning,*** *Mr. Jordan told his son the game gets more exciting.*

OR *Mr. Jordan told his son the game gets more exciting* ***after the sixth inning.***

LESSON 78: PARALLEL STRUCTURE

✎ **EXERCISE A (Page 244)**

1. *a* snowboarding
2. *b* for remodeled science labs
3. *b* cave exploring
4. *a* inexpensive
5. *b* took the dog to the kennel
6. *a* their significance

✎ **EXERCISE B (Page 245)**

1. *You may choose* ***either*** *the short-term mission trip or the summer survival camp.*
2. *Bach's "Little Fugue in G Minor" was a much harder piece for me to play than* ***for Ellie to play.***
3. *The sight in my left eye is better than* ***that in*** *my right eye.*
4. *Meals cooked at home are much tastier than* ***those cooked*** *in the hospital.*
5. *Growing up in South America is different than* ***growing up in*** *North America.*
6. *The view from Mt. Rainier, Washington, is even more awesome than* ***the view from*** *Mt. Whitney, California.*
7. *I talked to the president and* ***the*** *manager before I made my decision.*

OR *I talked to* ***both*** *the president* ***and the*** *manager before I made my decision.*

8. *Thad likes "diggling," the new bike-board sport, better than Chad* ***does.***
9. *George Washington led* ***not only*** *the colonial army but also the Constitutional Convention.*
10. *Jesus healed* ***both*** *the lame and the blind.*

LESSON 79: UNNECESSARY SHIFTS IN SENTENCES

✎ **EXERCISE (Page 248)**

1. *When* ***you*** *"Hike for Life,"* ***you*** *have an opportunity to demonstrate Christ's love to unborn children and their mothers.*

OR *When* ***Christians*** *"Hike for Life,"* ***they*** *have an opportunity to demonstrate Christ's love to unborn children and their mothers.*

2. *A young child must learn God's Word, obey his parents, and* ***pursue godly behavior.***
3. *When the rice comes to a boil, cover the pot and* ***reduce the heat.***
4. *Father* ***said*** *that we* ***were*** *all too emotional to think clearly when the family* ***began*** *to quarrel.*

OR *Father* ***says*** *that we* ***are*** *all too emotional to think clearly when the family* ***begins*** *to quarrel.*

5. *After* ***you*** *return from the retreat,* ***you*** *should start a Bible study for* ***your*** *own spiritual benefit.*

OR *After* ***the students*** *return from the retreat,* ***they*** *should start a Bible study for* ***their*** *own spiritual benefit.*

6. *Although he* ***planned*** *to go into business for himself, he* ***changed*** *his mind and* ***became*** *a CEO for IBM.*
7. ***Do*** *you like to read Reformation history or* ***is*** *the history of missions more appealing?*

OR *Do you like to read the* ***history of the Reformation*** *or the* ***history of missions****?*

LESSON 80: SENTENCE CONCISENESS

✎ **EXERCISE A (Page 249)** ***Answers will vary.***

1. *It goes without saying that you may add fuel to the fire with those remarks.*
2. *I think that liberal policies need to be exposed for what they are.*
3. *Harvey took a deep breath and stepped up to the podium at the Chicago Marriott Downtown.*
4. *"Diggling" has the potential to do to mountain biking what snowboarding did to skiing ten years ago.*
5. *When Melissa saw her thirteen-year-old brother driving the tractor, she was dumbfounded.*
6. *I asked Renee to reiterate what she said because it was inaudible.*
7. *As Sam read through the Bible, he was amazed by all the commands that God prescribed for His people to obey.*
8. *The course title* Applications of Grammar *means that, in our everyday writing and speaking, proper grammar should be practiced.*

✎ **EXERCISE B (Page 251)**

1. *After hearing the concert, I listened at home to three more cantatas* ***by Bach****.*
2. *Our drive in the Blue Mountains near* ***Sydney*** *would have been perfect if it had not been for our* ***flat*** *tire.*
3. *Our daughter,* ***the most adorable toddler this side of the Mississippi****, turned three today.*
4. ***After becoming paralyzed in a diving accident****, Joni Eareckson faced a* ***challenging*** *period of rehabilitation.*
5. ***While imprisoned in Scotland****, Samuel Rutherford,* ***a faithful pastor****, wrote hundreds of* ***insightful and sympathetic*** *letters.*
6. *The films directed by Alex Kirby dramatized* three ***Narnia*** *books, but not always* ***accurately****.*

LESSON 81: COMBINING AND REVISING SENTENCES

✎ **EXERCISE A (Page 255)**

Combine using *adjectives, adverbs,* and *prepositional phrases*:

1. *My kind friend encouraged me by listening.*
2. *Philip Emeagwali vigorously conducts research on next-generation supercomputers.*
3. *The angry girl threw the pillow at her sister.*

Combine using *introductory participial phrases*:

4. ***Sweeping across southern Florida****, the hurricane destroyed everything in its path.*

OR ***Destroying everything in its path****, the hurricane swept across southern Florida.*

5. ***Boarding the aircraft****, the computer consultant headed for Seattle.*

OR ***Headed for Seattle****, the computer consultant boarded the aircraft.*

6. ***Kneeling down with a towel****, Jesus washed the disciples' feet.*

Combine using *appositives*:

7. *The three friends climbed Mt. Everest,* ***the tallest mountain in the world with an elevation of 29,035 feet (8850 meters).***
8. *Jed Smith,* ***a trailblazer of the West****, was a Christian gentleman and the greatest of the mountain men.*
9. *John G. Paton,* ***a Scottish missionary to the New Hebrides****, gave to the Aniwan people their first hymnbook and translated the New Testament into their language.*

Combine using a *subordinate adverb clause*:

10. ***Because*** *parenting is a God-given responsibility, parents should use it to rear righteous children as God's Word directs.*
11. ***Although*** *thick fog blanketed the area, motorists kept driving.*
12. ***After*** *the hepatologist gazed at the blood tests thoughtfully, he quietly turned to the patient with liver disease.*

Combine using a *subordinate adjective clause*:

13. I forgot to bring the recipe which was lying on the kitchen counter.
14. Shannon wrote her research paper on Elector Frederick III of the Palatinate, whom she learned about on the Internet.
15. We met Mr. and Mrs. Ash, who had recently returned from the mission field in Indonesia.

✎ **EXERCISE B (Page 257)** ***Answers will vary.***

1. *When a survey was sent to registered voters asking them to indicate their greatest concern, national security was their first choice.*
2. *Philip decided to become a mathematician at age fourteen after mastering calculus. He could even out-calculate his instructors.*
3. *Iago, Shakespeare's most wicked villain, began to awaken suspicions in Othello, whose suspicions were ultimately converted into jealousy. Iago's reasons for hating various characters in the play were too obvious though muddled.*
4. *As Adam stood by Eve's side, he listened to Satan and ate the forbidden fruit.*
5. *Because it snowed the entire weekend, huge drifts of snow piled up around the house, preventing the Matthews from digging out for several days.*
6. *Since Martin, a competent programmer, had learned programming at Harper Community College, he was never out of work.*
7. *Speeding around the sharp turn, the Waverunner spun out of control and overturned in the water.*
8. *The extension of the suburban expressway is a subject of heated debate. Since the issues surrounding it seem insurmountable, the people do not anticipate any resolution soon.*

LESSON 82: UNIT REVIEW

✎ **EXERCISE A (Page 258)**

1. A sentence fragment is ***a group of words that is missing one or more of the parts needed to make a complete sentence***.
2. A complete sentence must have a ***subject*** and a ***verb*** and express a complete thought.
3. A ***phrase*** is a group of related words, containing neither a subject nor a predicate, and functions as a single part of speech.

4. A ***dependent*** clause does not express a complete thought and must not stand alone.
5. A ***run-on*** sentence is a grammatical error consisting of two or more sentences written as if they were only one.
6. List four ways the sentence described in number 5 can be corrected:
   a. ***Separate the sentences with a semicolon if the thoughts are closely related***.
   b. ***Separate the thoughts with a comma and coordinating conjunction if the thoughts are closely related***.
   c. ***Separate the thoughts into two sentences if the ideas are distinct***.
   d. ***Put one of the thoughts into a dependent clause if the ideas are closely related but not of equal grammatical rank***.
7. A coordinating conjunction is ***a word or group of words that link together words, phrases, or clauses of equal grammatical rank***.
8. The four common kinds of relationships between coordinate ideas are ***addition***, ***contrast***, ***choice***, and ***result***.
9. A subordinating conjunction is ***a word or group of words that connect a dependent (subordinate) clause to an independent clause***.
10. The four possible kinds of relationships between subordinate ideas and independent clauses are ***time***, ***cause or reason***, ***purpose or result***, and ***condition***.
11. List three ways faulty coordination can be corrected:
    a. ***Place the lesser idea in a subordinate adverb or adjective clause.***
    b. ***Place the lesser idea in a modifying phrase.***
    c. ***Place the lesser idea in an appositive.***
12. With respect to pronoun-antecedent agreement, define the three types of unclear references that should be avoided:

    Ambiguous: ***one in which the reader is unsure as to which of two possible antecedents the pronoun refers***.

    General: ***one in which a pronoun refers confusingly to a general idea in a phrase or clause, rather than to a specific antecedent***.

    Weak: ***one in which the antecedent has not been stated at all, but is assumed in the writer's mind***.
13. The ***indefinite*** use of pronouns, such as *it*, *they*, and *you* should be avoided in writing sentences.
14. ***Misplaced*** modifiers are those which are located in such a way that they appear to be modifying the wrong word.
15. What is the most common way to correct the modifier described in number 14?

    The most common way to correct a misplaced modifier is to move it next to, or closer to, the word it modifies.
16. List two ways the modifiers described in number 14 can be corrected:
    a. ***Move the misplaced modifier next to, or closer to, the word it modifies***.
    b. ***Move an adverb clause to the beginning of the sentence***.
17. ***Dangling*** modifiers are those which have no word in the sentence to logically modify; they are not logically connected to any word in the sentence.

18. What is the best way to correct the modifiers described in number 17?

    The best way to correct dangling modifiers is by adding a word that the phrase can logically modify, or by changing the phrase to an adverb clause by adding to it a subordinating conjunction and a subject and verb.

19. ***Two-way*** modifiers are those which cause confusion when they are placed in a position where they could *logically* modify two different words.

20. When two or more equal and closely related ideas are expressed in the same grammatical form in a sentence they are said to have ***parallel structure***.

21. List three ways parallel ideas in a sentence may be expressed in a parallel manner:

    a. ***When stating parallel ideas, repeat an article, a preposition, or a pronoun whenever necessary to make the meaning clear.***

    b. ***Place the correlative conjunctions both ... and; not only ... but also; neither ... nor; either ... or, immediately before the parallel items they introduce.***

    c. ***In the second part of a parallel construction add any word(s) necessary to make the parallelism clear and complete.***

22. What two unnecessary shifts in sentences result in an awkward style?

    a. ***Shifting from one subject to another***

    b. ***Shifting from one verb form to another***

23. State the two rules regarding verb-form shifting which you must always follow:

    a. ***Do not shift from active to passive voice or from passive to active voice within one sentence.***

    b. ***Do not shift from one verb tense to another within one sentence.***

24. What are two acceptable shifts of verb tense within a sentence?

    a. ***An appropriate shift from present tense to future tense or from past tense to future tense***

    b. ***When expressing a general truth such as a scientific or geographical fact***

25. What is the best way to change wordiness to conciseness in a sentence?

    The best way to change wordiness to conciseness in a sentence is by eliminating the unnecessary repetition of ideas and redundant words.

26. List three ways you can reduce a bulky sentence.

    a. ***Reduce clauses to participial, gerundial, or infinitive phrases.***

    b. ***Reduce clauses to appositives.***

    c. ***Reduce clauses and phrases to single words.***

Note: The following two questions deal with *style* rather than individual sentence *structure.*

---

27. How can *choppiness* be changed into a smooth and appealing style?

    a. ***Combine short sentences by adding adjectives, adverbs, prepositional phrases, participial phrases, or appositives.***

    b. ***Combine short sentences by putting one idea in a subordinate clause.***

28. How can a *stringy* style be changed into an interesting and logical one?

    a. ***Use subordinate clauses and participial phrases.***

    b. ***Divide stringy sentences into more than one sentence.***

✎ **EXERCISE B (Page 260)** ***This is how the article appeared in WORLD magazine, May 31, 2001.***

Venerable Vision[4]

by Linda Shrewsbury

5/31/2001

"The Buzz" in WORLD magazine

Black history month founder was pre-pc [politically correct]

When in 1926 black historian Carter G. Woodson instituted Negro History Week (the forerunner of today's Black History Month, celebrated across America every February), he wasn't kowtowing to the idols of multiculturalism. In fact, Woodson's hope of generating respect for the contributions of blacks to American society predated political correctness by more than half a century. Born into a poor Virginia family in 1875 (both his mother and father were former slaves), Woodson wasn't able to attend school regularly. Still, by age 17, he had mastered the fundamentals of common school subjects, largely through his own efforts.

For years, he toiled in Virginia's coal mines to help support his family. But at age 20, Woodson was able to enter high school, where he earned his diploma in less than two years. After earning a degree at Berea College in Kentucky, he worked as a teacher and writer and then earned a Ph.D. in history from Harvard University in 1912.

Woodson's studies convinced him that American history books ignored—and sometimes misrepresented—the black experience in this country. He set out to change that: In 1915, he founded the Association for the Study of Negro Life and History (which operates today as the Association for the Study of Afro-American Life and History). In 1916, he launched the *Journal of Negro History.* In 1921, he founded a publishing company to print books about black life that didn't interest mainstream publishers.

When he first conceived of Negro History Week, Woodson chose the second week in February to coincide with the birthdays of two persons who had dramatically affected the lives of black Americans: Abraham Lincoln and Frederick Douglass, the former slave who became a leading abolitionist. Fifty years later, during America's 1976 bicentennial celebration, the week-long observance was expanded to include the entire month.

This month marks the observance's diamond anniversary, but for many, Woodson's vision of greater respect and understanding between black and white Americans still seems far away.

---

4. This article may be found at World Journalism Institute's Web site under "who are we," under "student articles": <http://www.worldji.com/studentarticles.asp?news_id=91>

TEST KEY

TEST 1—UNIT 1

■ **Lessons 1-11**

Matching (48 pts)

1. F narrative
2. D expository
3. I description
4. A argumentative
5. C subject
6. H thinking
7. E topic
8. L clustering
9. G argument
10. J analogy
11. B composition
12. K brainstorming

Multiple Choice (52 pts)

13. tone
14. paragraph
15. worldview
16. transition
17. Observation
18. topic
19. proofreading
20. public
21. simple sentence
22. rounded development
23. summarizing
24. spatial
25. main idea

TEST 2—UNIT 1

■ **Lessons 1-11**

Multiple Choice (60 pts)

1. Narrative
2. causes
3. Incidents
4. unity
5. reasons
6. argumentative
7. definition
8. sequence
9. miscellaneous
10. deductive
11. information
12. division
13. particulars
14. both
15. proportion

Matching (40 pts)

16. B Appraising the first draft
17. C Writing the second draft
18. B Appraising the first draft
19. D Proofreading the second draft
20. D Proofreading the second draft
21. D Proofreading the second draft
22. E Writing the final draft
23. C Writing the second draft
24. A Writing the first draft
25. A Writing the first draft

TEST 3—UNIT 2

■ **Lessons 12-25**

Matching (40 pts)

1. B worldview
2. J parenthetical note
3. H clustering
4. D subject
5. I note taking
6. C tone
7. A main idea
8. E thesis statement
9. F general outline
10. G brainstorming

Multiple Choice (60 pts)

11. expository
12. both
13. Paraphrasing
14. eight-week
15. parenthetical
16. the truth
17. bibliography
18. creative
19. both
20. Plagiarism
21. limiting questions
22. documenting
23. audience
24. composition
25. Documentation

TEST 4—UNIT 3

■ **Lessons 26-33**

Matching (48 pts)

1. C argumentative
2. D persuasion
3. E informal guidelines
4. K plan of action
5. F sound argument
6. B rhetoric
7. H proposition
8. J evidence
9. A composition
10. L syllogism
11. G debatable issue
12. I opinion

Multiple Choice (52 pts)

13. inductive

Continued at the top of the next page.

14. major premise
15. deductive
16. presentation
17. logical inference
18. induction
19. the scientific method
20. analogy
21. both
22. minor premise
23. expressed opinion
24. Both
25. conclusion

TEST 5—UNIT 3

■ **Lesson 29**

Multiple Choice (60 pts)

1. arguing in a circle
2. begging the question
3. straw man
4. false analogy
5. false authority
6. bandwagon
7. false dilemma
8. card stacking
9. non-sequitur
10. slippery slope
11. hasty generalization
12. argue against the person
13. red herring
14. sweeping generalization
15. false cause

Matching (40 pts)

16. J hasty generalization
17. H false analogy
18. C false cause
19. F red herring
20. E non-sequitur
21. G card stacking
22. D false dilemma
23. I false authority
24. B begging the question
25. A arguing in a circle

TEST 6—UNIT 4

■ **Lessons 34-43**

Matching (48 pts)

1. E dash
2. B apostrophe
3. G hyphen
4. F exclamation point
5. H period
6. J comma
7. K quotation marks
8. I parentheses
9. C colon
10. D semicolon
11. A punctuation
12. L paragraph indentation

Multiple Choice (60 pts)

13. Brackets
14. spacing
15. Alignment
16. period
17. question mark
18. hyphen
19. dash
20. pauses in voice
21. neither one
22. neither one
23. 's
24. apostrophe
25. a hyphen

TEST 7—UNIT 5

■ **Lessons 44-52**

Matching (48 pts)

1. H simile
2. I metaphor
3. A trope
4. K alliteration
5. C metonymy
6. J personification
7. F hyperbole
8. L onomatopoeia
9. B synecdoche
10. E apostrophe
11. D oxymoron
12. G litotes

Multiple Choice (52 pts)

13. denotation
14. connotation
15. antithesis
16. homonyms
17. Synonyms, antonyms
18. Homographs
19. extended definitions
20. Description
21. Dialogue, monologue
22. character sketch
23. attribution
24. type sketch
25. paraphrasing

TEST 8—UNIT 6

■ **Lessons 53-59**

Multiple Choice (100 pts)

1. direct address
2. pronoun
3. noun
4. common, proper

Continued at the top of the next page.

5. single, compound
6. Collective
7. Reflexive, intensive
8. compound
9. antecedent
10. interrogative
11. substantive
12. Number
13. gender
14. Case
15. person
16. common
17. appositive
18. possessive
19. indefinite
20. possessive
21. nominative
22. objective
23. colloquies
24. brigadier generals
25. courtesies

TEST 9—UNIT 6

■ **Lessons 53-59**

Matching (48 pts)

1. B personal-possessive
2. D interrogative
3. I objective complement
4. H subject
5. C compound
6. E demonstrative
7. F indefinite
8. J predicate nominative
9. G relative
10. K appositive
11. A personal
12. L nounal gender

Multiple Choice (52 pts)

13. direct object
14. object of a preposition
15. indirect object
16. leader
17. book
18. nominative
19. objective
20. possessive
21. embargoes
22. both
23. nemeses
24. kin
25. both

TEST 10—UNIT 7

■ **Lessons 60-64**

Matching (40 pts)

1. E state-of-being
2. D helping
3. I imperative
4. C linking
5. B intransitive
6. G tone
7. A transitive
8. H indicative
9. F tense
10. J subjunctive

Multiple Choice (60 pts)

11. verb
12. coupling
13. helping
14. linking
15. Voice
16. verbals
17. Infinitives
18. Mood
19. participles
20. Gerunds
21. adjectives
22. principal parts
23. verb
24. verbal
25. subject

TEST 11—UNIT 7

■ **Lessons 60-64**

Matching (48 pts)

1. A present
2. I emphatic
3. C future
4. H progressive
5. J active
6. G simple
7. L past gerund
8. B past
9. D present perfect
10. E past perfect
11. F future perfect
12. K passive

Multiple Choice (52 pts)

13. gerund
14. participle
15. infinitive
16. both
17. infinitives
18. present
19. present participle
20. both
21. regular
22. irregular
23. both
24. emphatic
25. passive

TEST 12—UNIT 8

■ **Lessons 65-70**

Multiple Choice (100 pts)

1. interjection
2. adverb
3. conjunction
4. adjective
5. preposition
6. simple adjectives
7. compound preposition
8. subordinating
9. adjective
10. limit, definite
11. articles
12. preposition
13. conjunctive adverb
14. subordinating
15. Simple, correlative
16. adjectives
17. adverbs
18. adjectives
19. Simple
20. Correlative
21. predicate
22. appositive
23. objective
24. adverb
25. adjective

TEST 13—UNIT 9

■ **Lessons 71-73**

Multiple Choice (100 pts)

1. phrase
2. clause
3. prepositional
4. verb
5. participial
6. gerundial
7. infinitive
8. noun
9. adjective
10. adverb
11. prepositional
12. Verb
13. Participial
14. noun
15. Infinitives
16. signal words
17. clause
18. neither
19. Elliptical
20. infinitive
21. participial
22. gerundial
23. adjective
24. noun
25. adverb

TEST 14—UNIT 10

■ **Lessons 74-82**

Multiple Choice (100 pts)

1. dependent clause
2. phrase
3. run-on
4. phrase fragment
5. dependent clause fragment
6. run-on sentence
7. sentence fragment
8. indefinite
9. Misplaced
10. Dangling
11. Two-way
12. parallel
13. load
14. wordiness
15. conciseness
16. choppiness
17. stringy
18. subordinate
19. ambiguous
20. two-way
21. not parallel
22. subject
23. participial
24. clause
25. stringy

TEST 15—UNIT 10

■ **Lessons 74-82**

Multiple Choice (100 pts)

1. dangling
2. references
3. misplaced
4. either
5. misplaced
6. subordinating
7. dangling
8. neither
9. two-way
10. two-way
11. condition
12. choppy
13. reducing
14. sentence
15. sentence fragment
16. dependent clause fragment
17. run-on sentence
18. phrase fragment
19. weak
20. indefinite
21. parallel
22. verb tense
23. infinitive
24. result
25. adjective

Ad maiorem
Dei gloriam

Christian
502 West
Arlington Hei
www.christi

APEX
TP

781930367296

77084809 – 1